Pixel 7 For Seniors

An Easy to Understand Guide to Pixel and Android 13

Scott La Counte

ANAHEIM, CALIFORNIA

www.RidiculouslySimpleBooks.com

Table of Contents

Disclaimer: *Please note, while every effort has been made to ensure accuracy, this book is not endorsed by Alphabet, Inc. and should be considered unofficial.*

INTRODUCTION

The Pixel in many ways feels like the future of phones. Yes, the hardware is impressive, but it's the software that really makes it standout; the AI built inside it is arguably better than any phone out there.

But you probably aren't looking for a guy that tells you all about the AI; you want to learn how to take photos, make phone calls, and organize things. This book has you covered!

Whether you are switching from an iPhone or another Android device, this book is for you. It will break down everything you need to know about the device and keep it simple!

In this book, you'll learn about:

- Setting up your phone
- Making calls
- Installing apps
- Using the camera
- Surfing the Internet
- Changing system settings
- And much more!

The guide is based off of *The Insanely Simple Guide to Android 13* but has a bonus book on using Gmail that I think you'll find useful.

Ready to learn more? Let's get started!

[1] START HERE

PIXEL VS PIXEL

The interesting thing about the next generation of Pixel–indeed with all of their phones–is often found in the software, not their hardware. Where Google arguably shines over the competition is with the AI built into the software–AI that comes first to the latest generation phone, and sometimes doesn't make it at all to the older phones. With the Pixel 7, the AI enhancement is strongest with what it can do for your photos (more on that later).

That said, there are some enhancements to the Pixel 7 over last years Pixel 6.

The price, thankfully, hasn't changed on the Pixel; the colors, however, have--as they usually do on the Pixel. Cosmetics-wise, the Pixel is also slightly lighter and thinner. The actual screen size is also just a smidgen smaller, which you probably won't notice. Face Unlock is also back on the Pixel--this feature has been missing since the Pixel 4; you still have the option, however, to unlock the phone with a fingerprint.

Processor-wise, the phone is faster; it has an upgraded Tensor G2 chip–something casual users, might not notice, but will make your phone run more smoothly in the background.

The camera is what everyone wants to know, though! While the front camera did get upgraded to 10.8 MP (up from 8MP on the 6), the back camera is unchanged. That's not the same with the Pro series phone, which has a ultra wide lens and better zoom.

Here's one thing to consider when your considering making an upgrade from the Pixel 6 to 7: Google gives a very fair buyback on phones at launch. Trading in your Pixel 6 to a Pixel 7 will cost you probably less than $200 (buy back range changes over time).

PIXEL VS IPHONE VS SAMSUNG

The real question for a lot of people isn't how the Pixel stacks up against itself, rather how it stacks up against other flagship phones–notably the iPhone and Samsung S series.

So, how does it stand up? In a word: fantastic! All the flagship phones have features that make them stand out; you can debate all day which one has the better camera or processor or apps, but one thing is clear about the Pixel: it is, by far, the best bang for your buck. Google prices the phones quite aggressively against the competition, and for the money, you are getting a top of the line phone for a price that's much cheaper than others.

But let's look closer at how they actually compare.

Looking at the weight of the phones, Pixel is the heaviest of the bunch (starting at 197 grams); the Samsung S22 is the lightest (starting at 168 grams); chances are, you won't notice.

On paper the cameras all look very different; on the base iPhone (not the pro), the camera is 12 MP; the Pixel and Samsung phone are 50 MP. But don't rely on paper alone when you are talking about cameras; even at 12MP, many will argue the iPhones photos are better. It's really the lens and how the photos are processed that make them good. The iPhone does top both the Samsung and Pixel with its front lens--12 MP vs 10.8 on the Pixel and 10 on the Samsung.

Both the Pixel and iPhone can capture 4K video; the S22 tops them with the ability to shoot in 8K--both, again, that doesn't mean it's a better video camera; also, keep in mind, most TVs do not currently have 8K, so even if you take a 8K video, you'll have a hard time finding a place to show it.

The internal memory on the phones are hard to compare because iPhone does not disclose how much RAM is on the iPhone 14.

Both the Pixel and Samsung use USB-C; the iPhone still relies on a lightening adapter, which disappoints so people who want one charger to charge all things.

[2]
Setting Up

This chapter will cover:

- Setup
- Face unlock
- Main user interface elements

SETUP

The setup is pretty intuitive, but there are still screens that might confuse you a little. If you are a self-starter and like just try things, then skip to the next section on the main UI elements of Android. If you want a more thorough walk-through, then read away!

Google knows you want to get started using your phone, so they've made the process pretty quick; most people will spend about 5 or 10 minutes.

The first thing you'll see is the "Hi there" screen; you could technically make an emergency call on this screen, but I don't recommend it unless it's really an emergency—this isn't a "hey, mom, I'll be late" emergency...this is a direct to emergency responders "I've fallen and can't get up" sort of call. When you are ready to get started, tap the blue "Start" button.

You have two options on the next screen: connect to wi-fi so you can start a "SIM-free" setup or insert your SIM card.

If you add a SIM card you can skip all of the next steps. If you are doing SIM-Free, then tap "Start SIM-free setup instead." The next screen explains SIM-free; SIM-free is exactly what it sounds like, but it's not supported by all carriers. If your carrier supports it, then I'd recommend doing it, as everything will be stored online vs. on a card that can be easily scratched and damaged. Tap the blue "Next" to begin.

SIM-free setup

If your mobile network uses SIM-free setup, you'll get calls, texts, and data by downloading an eSIM instead of inserting a SIM card.

The next screen prompts you to select your wi-fi network. This is followed by an update screen. It should take about a minute to get the latest update. When it's done, you'll see the "Copy apps & data" screen.

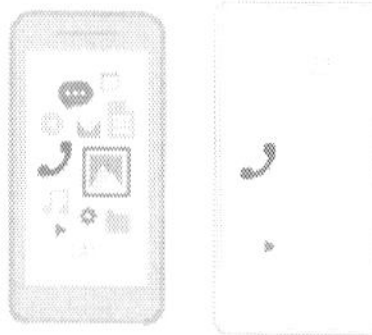

Copy apps and data is pretty resourceful. It will let you copy everything from your old phone so there's not as much to do on your new one—it works with both iPhone (through a special adaptor) and Android. It's not perfect—especially with the iPhone—but it will save you time. If you are coming from a previous generation Android phone, you can also do this without a cord by using your login. If you want to skip it and start from scratch, then select "Don't copy" in the lower left corner.

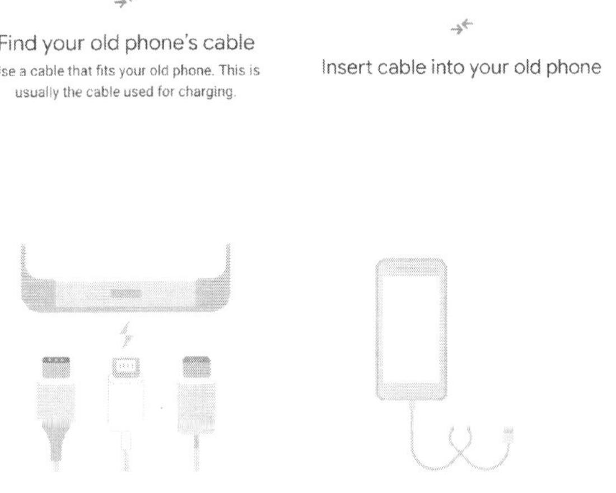

Find your old phone's cable
Use a cable that fits your old phone. This is usually the cable used for charging.
Insert cable into your old phone

Next, sign in to your Google Account (the one you use the check email usually—unless you don't use Gmail). If you don't have a Google Account, then click the option to create it.

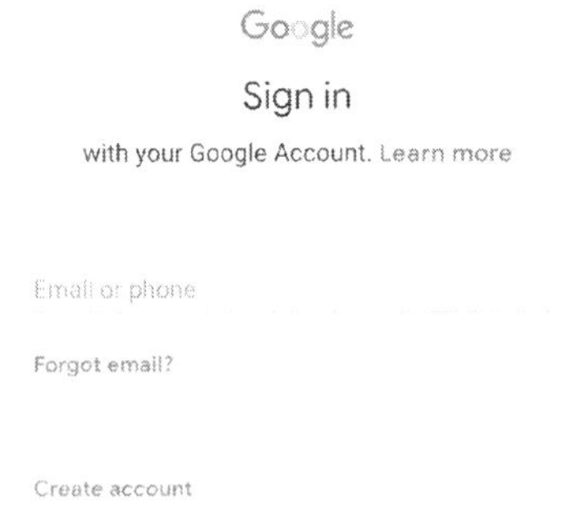

Once you hit "next" and "sign in," you'll get a bunch of legal stuff. It's basically saying Google's not responsible for anything. Agree to it or you just bought yourself a very expensive brick. You'll see a lot of these legal screens, so either put on your reading glasses and settle in for a very long night, or just agree to them.

Google Services is the next screen. This is giving the phone permission to use features on the phone (like the fingerprint scanner, location services to see where you are at, send Google and developers crash reports, and backup your phone to the Google Drive). I recommend selecting all of them. If you are worried about privacy, I'll show you some adjustments you can make later. I should also note: if you turn them off here, you can turn them back on later.

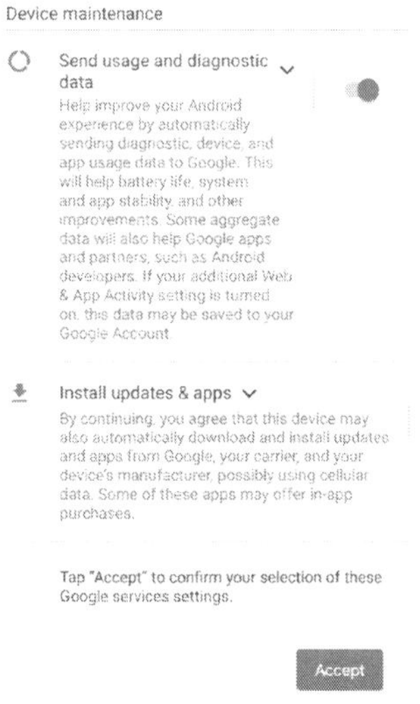

Next is yet another reminder that you can't blame Google for anything. They really want you to understand this. That way if the phone explodes in your hand, it's obviously your fault!

G

Additional legal terms

By clicking "I accept," you agree to the Google Terms of Service and the Google Device Arbitration Agreement.
Note: The Google Privacy Policy describes how your data is handled.

All disputes regarding your Google device will be resolved through **binding arbitration** on an individual, non-class basis, as described in the Google Device Arbitration Agreement, unless you opt out by following the instructions in that Agreement.

Next, it's time to start setting up your phone. What was all that other stuff? That was your account. First up to bat: your screen lock. This is basically so if someone steals or finds your phone, they can't open it unless they know your password.

Set screen lock

For security, set PIN

PIN must be at least 4 digits

Screen lock options

If you tap on "Screen lock options" you will see even more options. The unlock can be a pattern (e.g. move in the shape of a seven), it can be a word, or it could be a number (but don't use your bank pin number!). You can also skip adding a pin and have your phone always unlocked.

The next screen will ask you for a pin. If you tap "Screen lock options" you can also add a pattern. It's all a preference. My only advice is not to use a pin you use somewhere else (like a bank pin) or an easy pin (like 1234).

Once you hit "Next," and then reenter the pin to confirm it.

You'll also have the option for adding a fingerprint to unlock your phone. Unlike a lot of phones, the Pixels fingerprint sensor is on the screen itself. Pretty cool right? Here's a nugget of advice, however. If you are like me, you'll probably put a screen protector over it so there's more protection if it falls. That's going to be problematic for your sensor until you update it—so if you are finding it's not working, then update the Android software (I'll show you how later) and see if that fixes it.

Adding a finger print is pretty simple. The phone will tell you exactly where your finger should go. Just tap your finger to the screen where shown. That's it! You can add one finger or several. You can also add other people's fingers—so if you have someone who you give permission to use your phone, then you can add them as well.

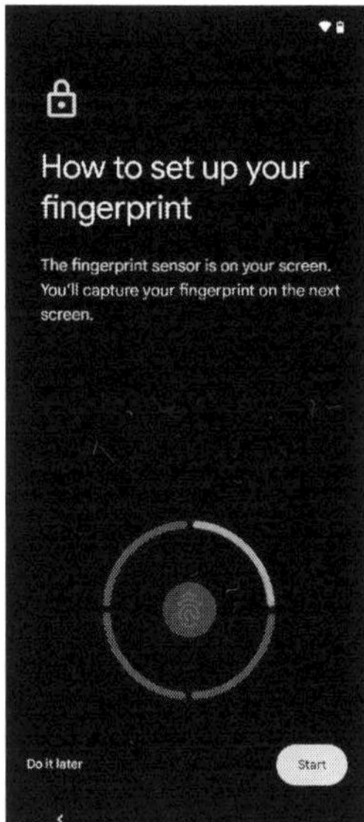

Just tap Add Another at the end of the setup if you want to add more.

New to Pixel 7 is the ability to unlock with your face; this is something that's been missing sense the Pixel 4.

Configuring Google Assistant is next. Google Assistant is the Google equivalent of Siri. You can tap "Leave & get reminder" but it's very quick to do, so it's best to just get it out of the way.

Make Pixel uniquely yours
Keep going to set up your Google Assistant, change your wallpaper, and more. Or, leave now and finish later.

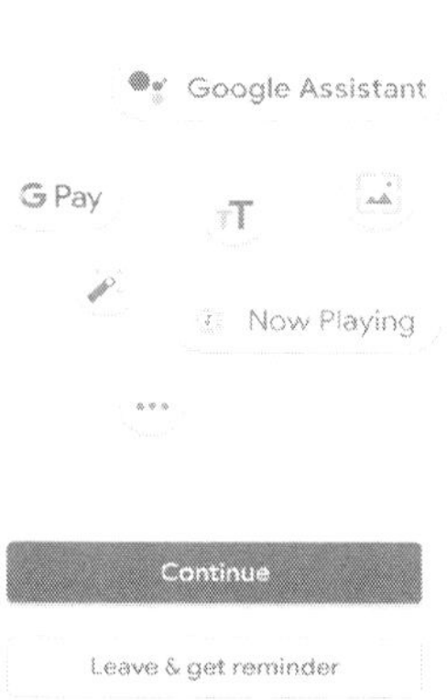

Once you agree to the terms, you are ready to go. You'll be asked a few questions (unless you have a Google Home and Google already knows your voice).

You are just about done! The "Anything else?" screen is your last chance to add in settings before finishing the set up—and remember: you can change all this later. So if you don't want to do it now, you always can do it later. The one thing I will point out is "Add another email account"; if you are using this phone at work, then it's a good idea to add in your work email here.

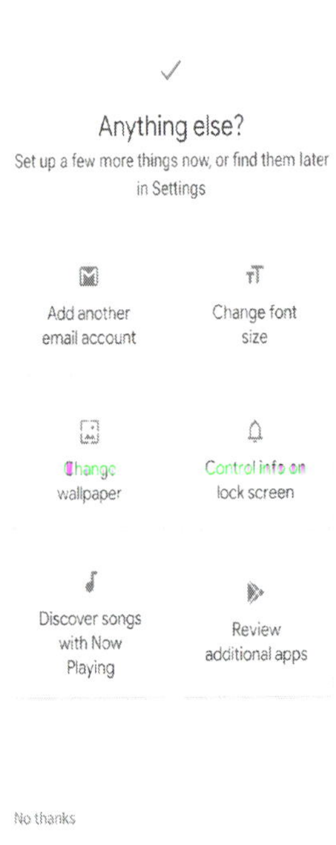

The last screen is asking if you'd like to get tip emails from Google about how to use your phone. When you are first getting started, these emails are helpful. They don't come very often. If you want to turn it on, then just toggle the "sign up" button to on (it will turn blue—or be blue if it's already checked).

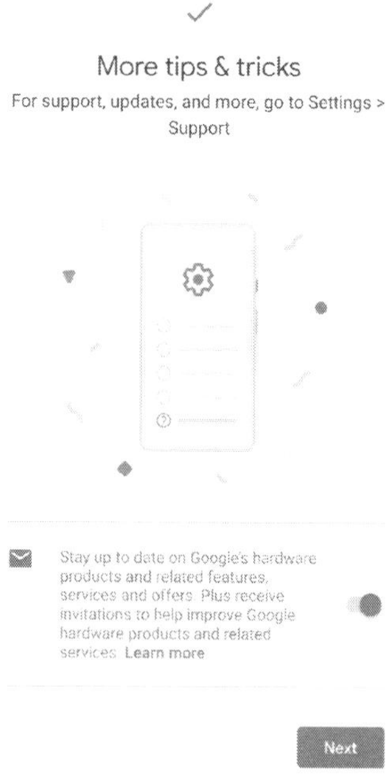

More tips & tricks
For support, updates, and more, go to Settings > Support
Stay up to date on Google's hardware products and related features, services and offers. Plus receive invitations to help improve Google hardware products and related services. Learn more
Next

After a few seconds, a screen will appear that says, "Go Home." Kind of sounds like the phone is telling you that you didn't pass the setup and now must go home empty handed.

Don't worry! It's just telling you to go to the Home screen because you are finally done. These final screens are short tutorials that will give you a couple tips for how the phone works.

After a few tips, you'll see the "All set!" screen, which is the final screen. You are finally done!

Swipe up and you will see your Home screen. You are finally ready to use your phone!

FINDING YOUR WAY AROUND

People come to the Pixel from all sorts of different places: iPhone, other Android phone, flip phone, two styrofoam cups tied together with string. This next section is a crash course in the interface. If you've used Android before, then it might seem a little simple, so skip ahead if you already know all of this.

If any of this seems a little rushed, there's good reason: it is! We'll cover these points in more detail later. This is just a quick starter / reference.

On the bottom of your screen is the shortcut bar—you'll be spending a lot of time here; you can add whatever you want to this area, but these are the apps Google thinks you'll use most—and, with the exception of the Play Store, they are probably right. Depending on the settings you've picked and the phone you have, it may or may not look different. It could show four apps in a row instead of six, for example.

So, what are these? Real quick, these are as follows:

- **Phone**: Do you want to take a wild guess what the phone button does? If you said brings you an ice cream, then maybe you aren't cut out for a phone. But if you said something along the lines of "It launches an app to call people" then you'll have no problem at all with your new device. Surprise, surprise: this pricey gadget that plays games, takes pictures, and keeps you up to date on political ramblings on social media does one more interesting thing: it calls people!
- **Message**: Message might be a little more open-ended than "Phone"; that could

mean email message, text messages, messages you keep getting on your bathroom mirror to put the toilet seat down. In this case, it means "text messages" (but really—put that toilet seat down...you aren't doing anyone any favors). This is the app you'll use whenever you want to text cute pictures of cats.

- **Play Store**: Anything with the word "Play" in the title must be fun, right?! This app is what you'll use to download all those fun apps you always hear about.
- **Chrome**: Whenever you want to surf the Internet, you'll use Chrome. There are actually several apps that do the same thing—like Firefox and Opera—but I recommend Chrome until you are comfortable with your phone. Personally, I think it's the best app for searching the Internet, but you'll soon learn that most things on the phone are about preference, and you may find another Internet browser that suits your needs more.
- **Camera**: This apps opens pictures of vintage cameras...just kidding! It's how you take pictures on your phone. You use this same app for videos as well.

Next to the shortcut bar, the area you'll use the most is the notification bar. This is where you'll get, you guessed it, notifications! What's a notification? That's any kind of notice you have elected to receive. A few examples: text message alerts, email alerts, amber alerts, and apps that have updates.

When you drag your finger down from the notification bar, you'll get a list of several settings that you can adjust. Press and hold any of these options and you'll open an app with even more options.

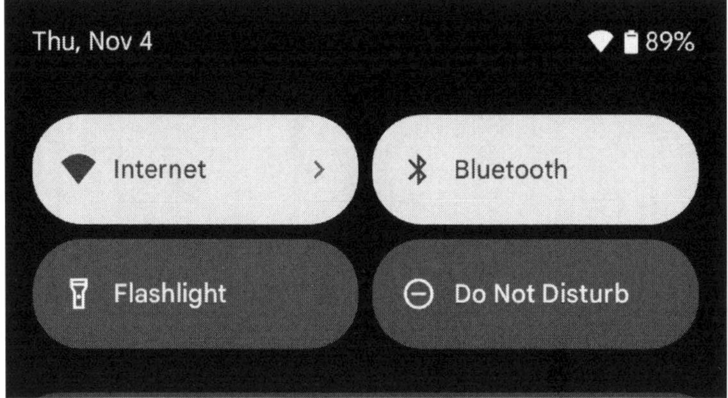

From right to left these are the options you can change or use:

- Wi-fi
- Bluetooth
- Do not disturb
- Flashlight

If you continue dragging down, this thin menu expands and there are a few more options.

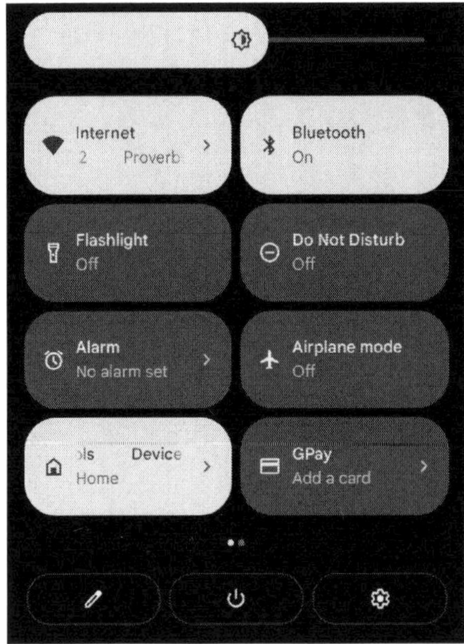

The first is at the top of the screen—it's the slider, and it makes your device brighter or dimmer depending on which way you drag it.

You can slide your finger to see more options:

- Auto-Rotate – Locks (unlocks) the device from rotating
- Battery Saver – Puts the device in a low energy mode for extended battery life, but not as great processing power.
- Screen cast – Beams the screen to another device—like a Google TV.
- Screen Record – Screen recording used to be something you needed a special app for; Android 11 brought native recording. So you can record what you are doing on your screen and share it with someone

else. It's great for tutorial videos. You are also able to use your phone's microphone to narrate with your voice.

- Nearby share
- Camera / Mic Disable – Quickly turn off your camera or mic.

Near the bottom on the left, is a little pencil edit button. That let's you reorganize what options are shown where.

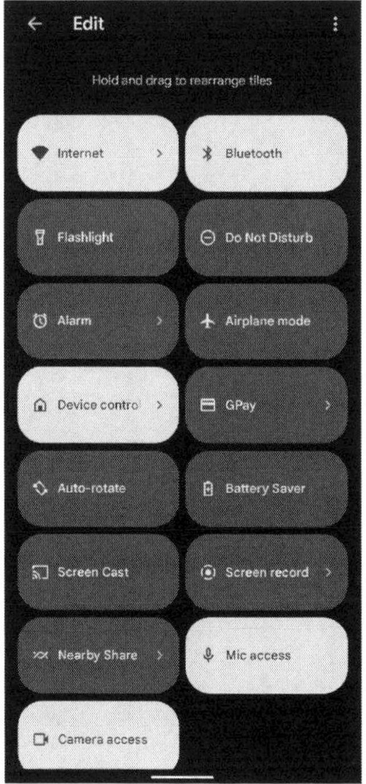

Scroll a little more and you'll see even more quick settings that you can add to the notification bar. Among them:

- **Data** – Tapping this turns your data on and off, which is handy if you are running low on data and don't want to be charged extra for it.
- **Night light** - This is a special mode that dims your screen and makes the screen appropriate for reading in dark settings.
- **Battery share** – when you press this, you can use your device like a wireless charger. What does that mean? Let's say your friend has an iPhone with wireless charging and they're almost out of battery. You can press this, then hold their phone against yours and share your battery wirelessly with them.

Something else that's pretty cool on this notification area: you can see a history of notifications.

If you get a lot of notifications, you probably have accidentally dismissed something that you didn't mean to. Now you can see what it was.

To use it, go to the bottom of all your notifications, then select "Manage."

From here, toggle "Use notification history" to on.

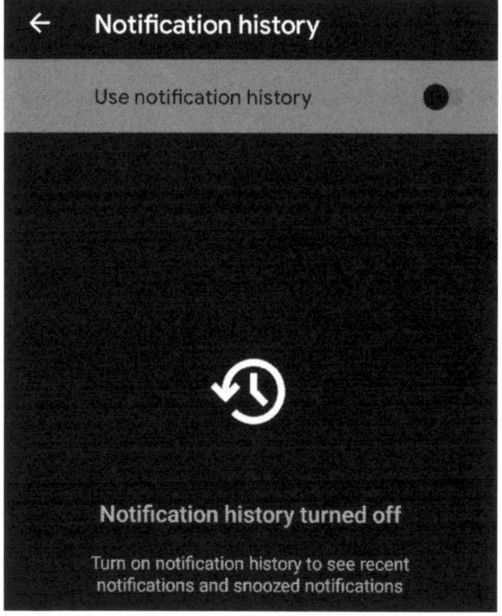

Now when you go back to that same area "Manage" is replaced with "History."

FEELING HOME-LESS?

You may have noticed something that seems important missing from your phone: a Home button. On older phones, this was a critical button that gets you to the Home screen whenever you push it.

How on Earth do you get Home without a Home button?! Easy. Are you ready? Swipe up. That's it!

If you've used any Apple device, then you might know a thing or two about Siri. She's the assistant that "sometimes" works; Google has its own version of Siri and it's called Google Assistant. The names not quite as creative as Siri, but many say it works better. I'll let you be the judge of that.

To get to the Google Assistant from anywhere, just say "Ok, Google." If you are on the Home screen, then there's also a Google Assistant widget. This little bar does more than make appointments and get your information—it's also a global search. What does that mean? It means you can type in anything you want to know, and it will search both the Internet and your phone. If it's a contact in your phone, then it will get you that. But if it's the opening hours for the Museum of Strange then it will search the Internet—it will also give you a map of the location and the phone number.

GET AROUND ON YOUR PIXEL PHONE

When it comes to getting around your Pixel, learning how to use gestures will be the quickest, most effective method. You can change some of the gesture options by going to the Settings app, then System > Gestures > System navigation.

The most important gesture is how to get back to the Home screen—there are no buttons after all. That's the easiest one to remember: swipe up from the bottom of the screen.

When you are on an Internet page, you can swipe from the left or right edge of the screen to go backwards or forwards.

To select text, tap and hold over the text, then lift your finger when it responds.

MULTITASKING

Those are the easy gestures to remember; if you want to move around quickly, however, you need to know the two big multitask gestures, which help you switch between apps.

The first is to see your open apps. To do this, swipe up like you're going to the Home screen, but keep going until about the middle of the screen and then stop and lift your finger—don't make a quick swipe-up gesture like you would when going Home. This will show you previews of all of your open apps, and you can swipe between them. Tap the one you want to open.

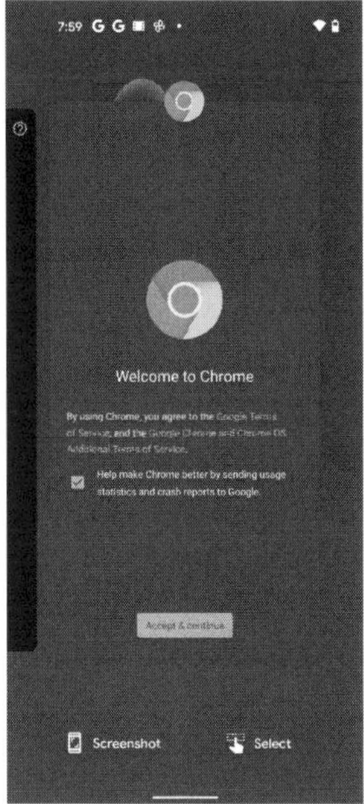

The quickest way to switch back and forth between two or three apps, however, is to swipe from left to right along the bottom edge of the screen. This swipes between apps in the order that you have used them.

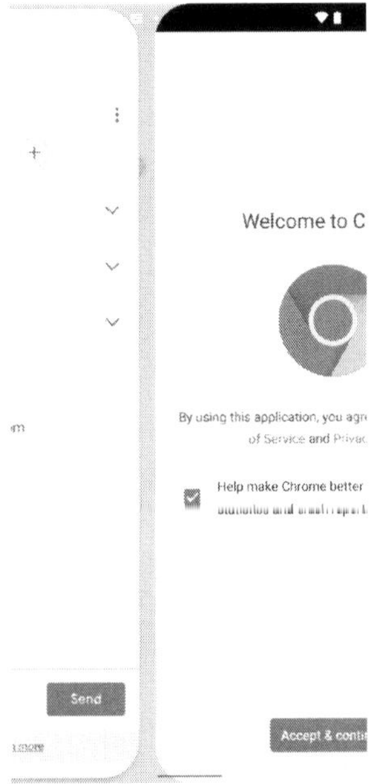

ZOOM

Need to see text bigger? There are two ways to do that. Note: this works on many, but not all apps.

The first way is to pinch to zoom.

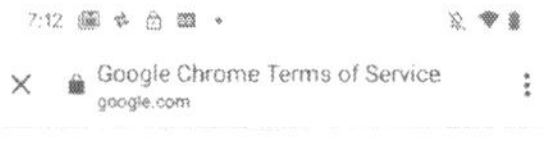

The second way is to double tap on the text.

Rotate

You probably have noticed if you rotate your phone, it rotates the screen. What if you don't want to rotate the entire screen? You can turn that off very easily. Swipe down and then tap the "arrows" button to enable or disable it.

[3]

The Ridiculously Simple Overview of All the Things You Should Know

This chapter will cover:

- Customizing screens
- Split screens
- Gestures

MAKING PRETTY SCREENS

If you've used an iPhone or iPad, then you may notice the screen looks a little...bare. There's literally nothing on it. Maybe you like that. If so, then good for you! Skip ahead. If you want to decorate that screen with shortcuts and widgets, then read on. Since Android 12 made things more about you than ever before, prepare to have more control than ever before!

ADDING SHORTCUTS

Any app you want on this screen, just find it, and then press and hold; when a menu comes up, drag it upward until the screen appears and move it to where you want it to go. You can also drag it to new screens.

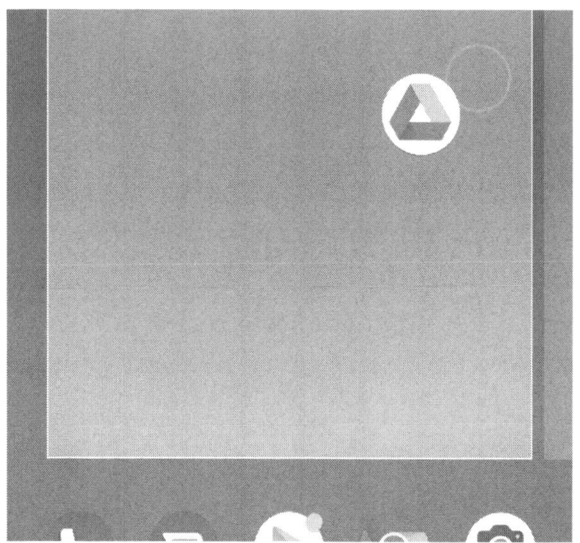

To remove an app from a screen, tap and hold, then drag it upward to the "Remove" text that appears when you move it up. When it's there, let go.

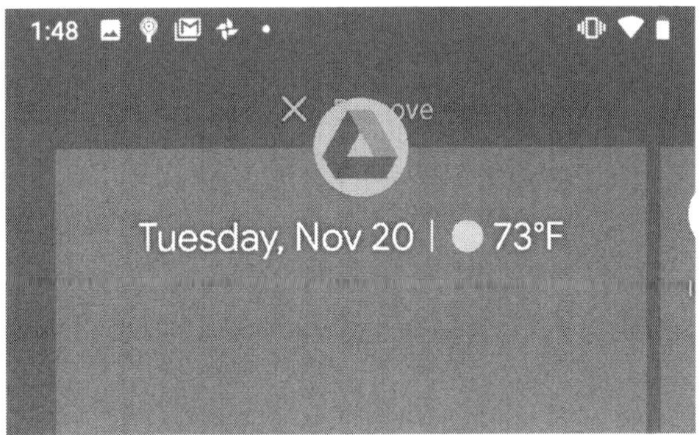

WIDGETS

Shortcuts are nice, but widgets are better. Widgets are sort of like mini-programs that run on your screen. A common widget people put on their screen is the weather forecast. Throughout the day the widget will update automatically with up-to-date info.

To add a widget, go to the screen you want to add it to and tap and hold until the menu comes up.

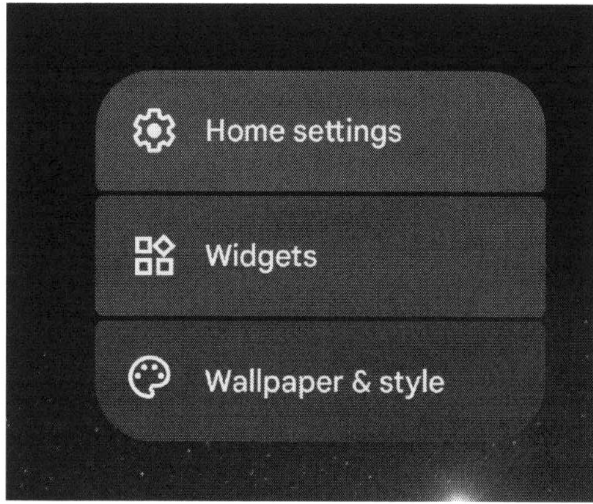

Select "Widgets." This opens up a widget library—it's like a mini app store.

When you find one you want to add, tap and hold it, then drag it to the screen you want to add it to.

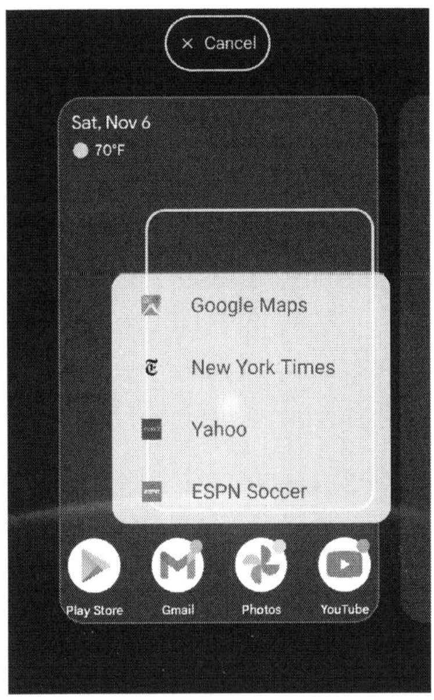

Widgets come in all sorts of shapes and sizes, but most of them can be resized. To resize it, tap and hold it. If you see little circles, then you can tap those and drag it in or out to make it bigger or smaller.

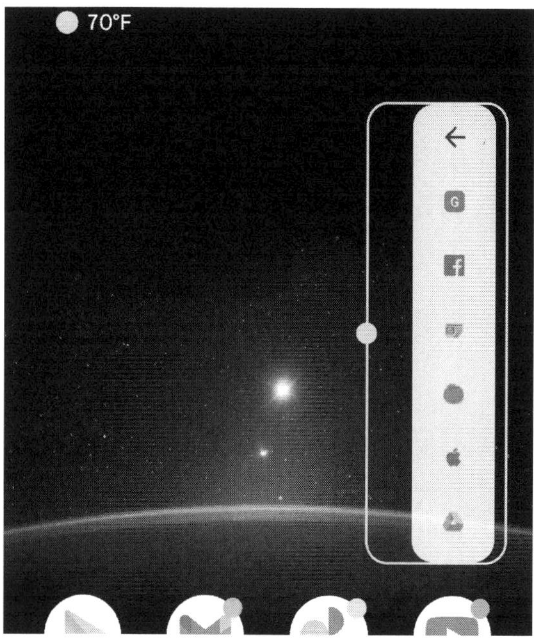

You remove widgets the same way you remove shortcuts. Tap and hold and then drag it upward to the remove.

WALLPAPER

Adding wallpaper to your screen is done in a similar way. Tap and hold your finger on the Home screen, when the menu comes up, select "Wallpaper" instead of "Widgets." Some of the options even move—so the wallpaper always has something moving across your screen—it's like a slow moving movie.

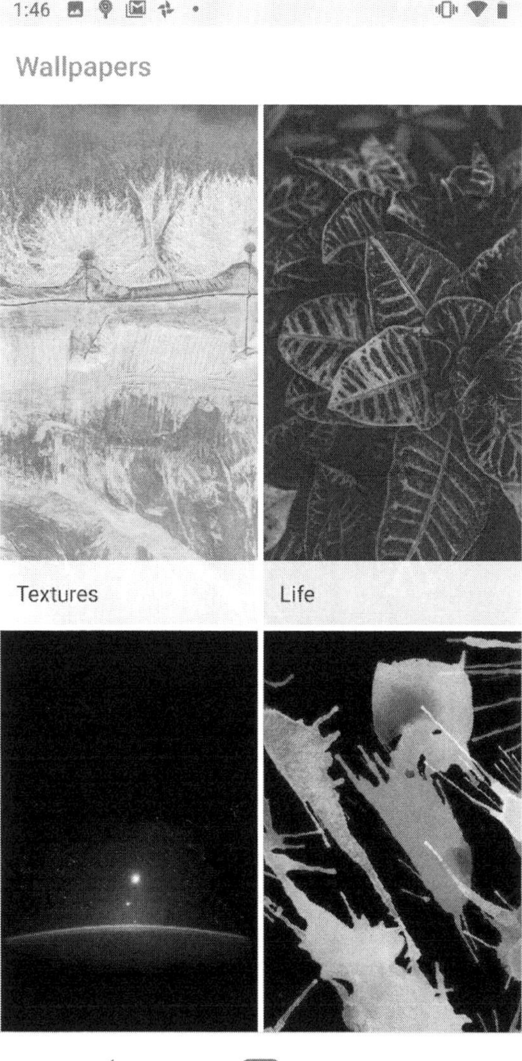

When you have a wallpaper open that you want to add, just hit the "Set Wallpaper" in the upper right corner.

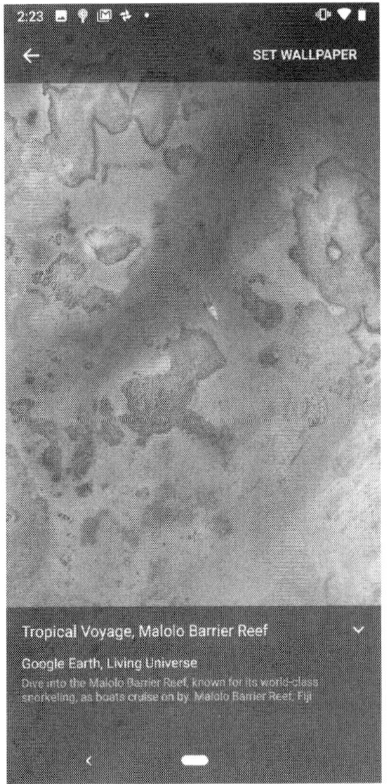

You can also change the style of your phone—such as the colors.

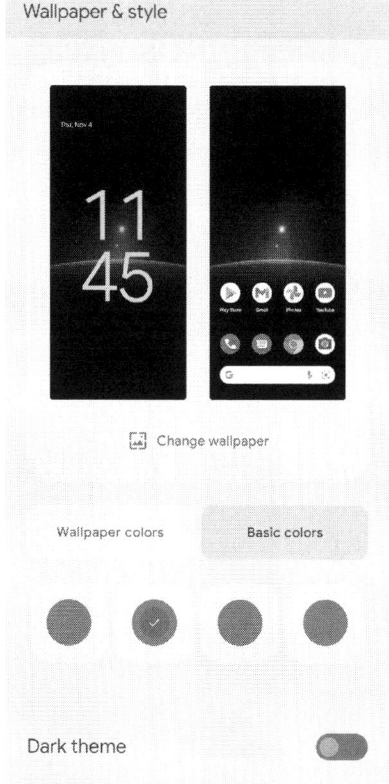

A WORD, OR TWO, ABOUT MENUS

It's pretty intuitive that if you tap on an icon, it opens the app. What's not so obvious is if you tap and hold there are other options. Every app is different. Usually, they're shortcuts—tapping and holding over the Phone icon, for example, brings up your favorites; doing the same thing over the camera brings up a selfie mode shortcut. Tap and hold over your favorite apps to see what shortcuts are available.

SPIT SCREENS

The Pixel phone comes in two different sizes; the bigger screen obviously gives you a lot more space, which makes split screen apps a pretty handy feature. It works on the smaller Pixel as well, though it doesn't feel as effective on the smaller screen.

To use this feature, swipe up to bring up multitasking; next, tap the icon above the window you want to turn into split screen (note: this feature is not supported on all apps); if split screen is available, you'll see a menu that has an option for split screen.

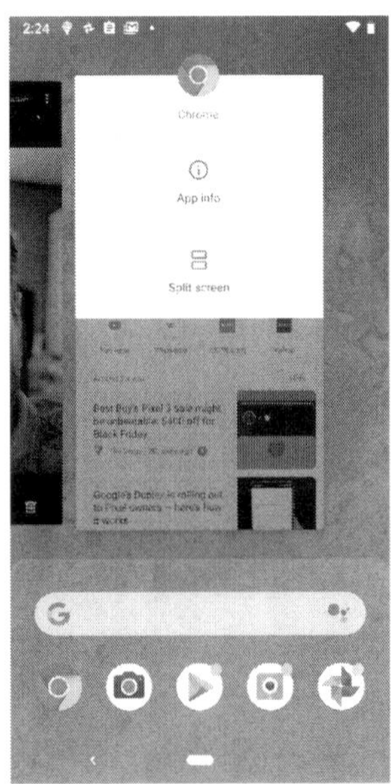

Once you tap "split screen," it will let you swipe left and right to find the app you want to split the screen with. Tap the one you want.

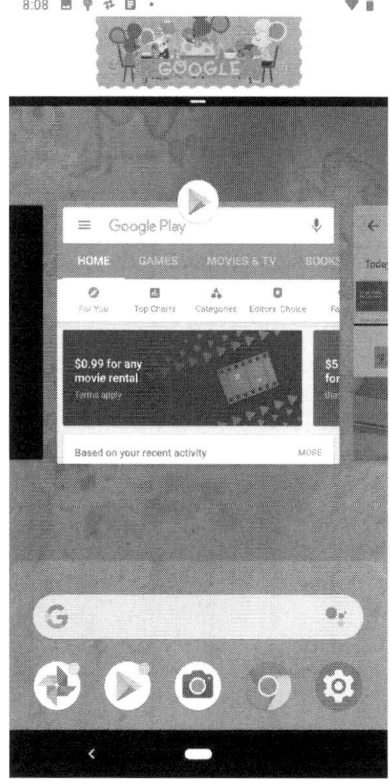

Your screen is now split in two.

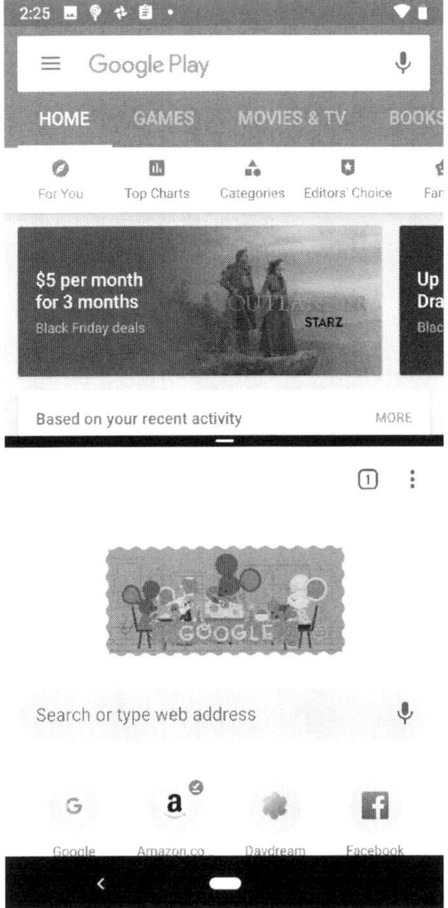

That thin black bar in the middle is adjustable; you can move it up or down so one of the apps has more screen real estate.

To exit this mode, drag the black bar either all the way to the top or all the way to the bottom until one of the apps completely goes away.

GESTURES

Jump to Camera

Press the power button twice to quickly jump to the camera.

Flip Camera

Switch in and out of selfie mode while you are in the camera by double-twisting the phone.

Double-tap

If your phone is in standby, double-tap the screen and the time and notifications will appear.

Google Assistant

Google Assistant can be trigged by saying "Hey, Google". With gestures, there's a new way: swipe from either the right or left bottom corner.

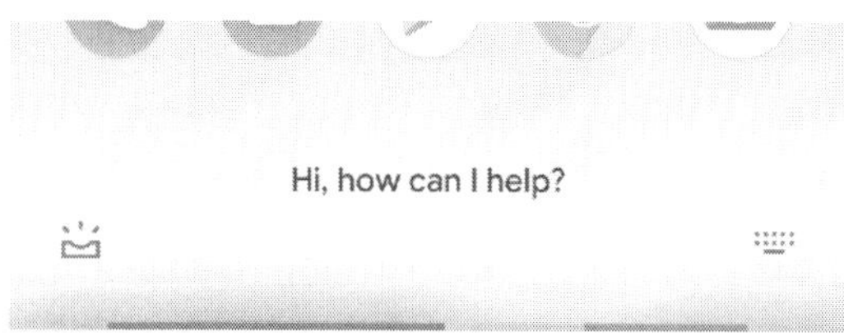

[4]
The Basics...and Keep It Ridiculously Simple

This chapter will cover:
- Making calls
- Sending messages
- Finding and downloading apps
- Driving directions

Now that you have your phone set up and know your way around the device at its most basic level, let's go over the apps you'll be using the most that are currently on your shortcut or favorite bar:

- Phone
- Messages

- Google Play Store
- Chrome

Notice that Camera is off this list? There's a lot to cover with Camera, so I'll go over it in a separate chapter.

Before we get into it, there's something you need to know: how to open apps not on your favorite bar. It's easy. From your home screen, swipe up from the bottom. Notice that menu that's appearing? That's where all the additional apps are.

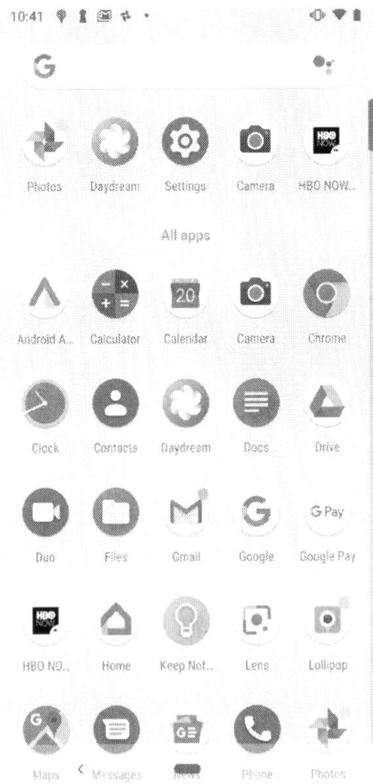

MAKING CALLS

So...who you going to call? Ghostbusters?!

You would be the most awesome person in the world if Ghostbusters was in your phone contacts! But before you can find that number in your contacts, it would probably help to know how to add a contact, find a contact, edit a contact, and put contacts into groups, right? So before we get to making calls, let's do baby steps and cover Contacts.

CONTACTS

So, let's open up the Contacts app to get started. See it? Not on your favorite bar, right? So where is it?! That's why I showed you earlier how to get to additional apps. Swipe up from the bottom of your screen and keep swiping until the menu appears in its entirety.

It's in alphabetical order, so the Contacts app is in the C's. It looks like this:

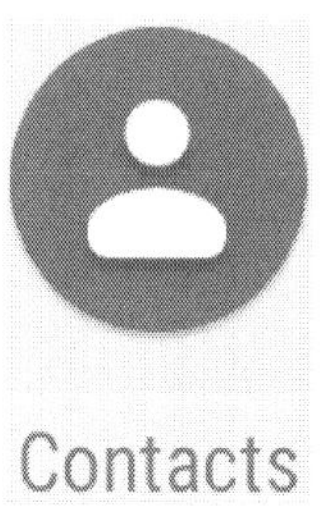

Chances are if you've added your email account, you'll already have a lot of contacts listed. Like hundreds!

You can either scroll slowly, or head to the right-hand side of the app and scroll—this lets you quickly scroll by letters. Just slide your finger until you see the letter of the contact you want and then stop.

I'm getting ahead of myself, however! Before you can scroll, it would be nice to know how to add a contact so there are people to scroll to. To add a contact, tap on that blue plus sign.

Adding a person looks more like applying for a job than adding a contact. There are rows and rows of fields!

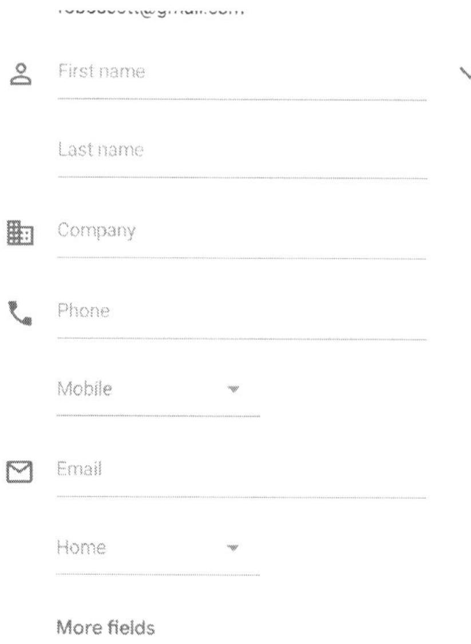

Just in case you weren't overwhelmed by all the fields, you can tap more fields and get even more!

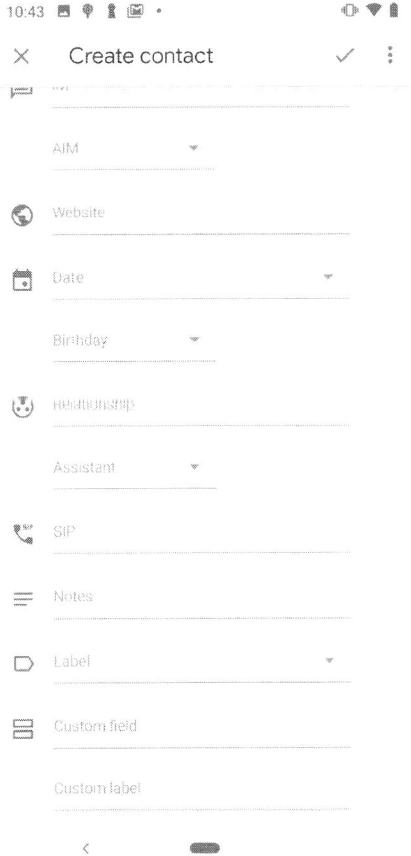

Is that not enough? Google has you covered because you can add a custom field!

Here's the most important thing you need to know: fields are optional! You can add a name and email and that's it. You don't even have to add their phone number. If you want to call them, then that would certainly help though.

If you have a hard time remembering who people are, then you can also take a picture or add a picture you already have. Comes in handy if you have eight kids and you can't remember if Joey is the one with blonde hair or red hair.

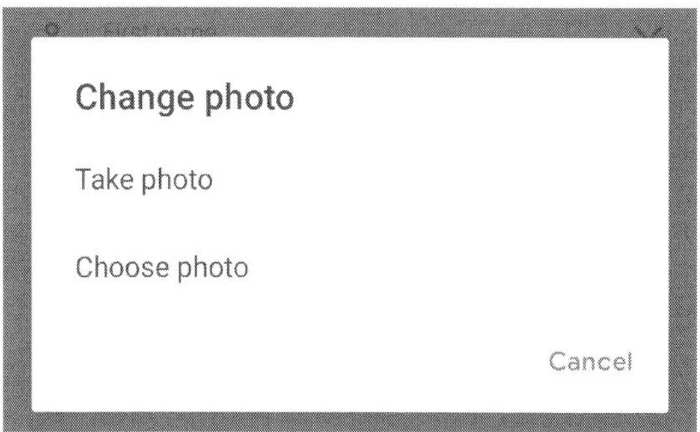

Once you are done, tap the checkbox. That saves it. If you decide you don't want to add a contact after all, the tap the X. That closes it without saving.

Editing a Contact

If you add an email and then later decide you should add a phone number, or if you want to edit anything else, then just find the name in your contacts and tap it once. This brings up all the info you've already added.

Go to the lower corner and tap on the pencil button. This makes the contact editable. Go to your desired field and update. When you are finished, tap the checkbox in the upper right corner.

Sharing a Contact

If you have your phone long enough, someone will ask you for so and so's phone number. The old-fashioned way was to write it down. But you have a smartphone, so you aren't old-fashioned!

The new way to share a number is to find the person in your contacts, tap their name, then tap those three dots in the upper right corner of your screen. This brings up a menu.

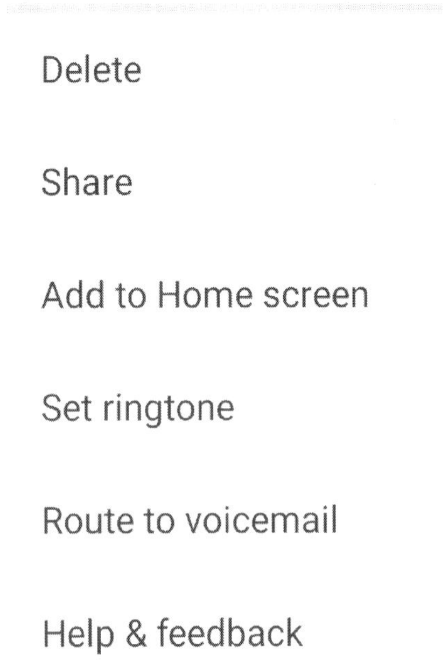

Delete

Share

Add to Home screen

Set ringtone

Route to voicemail

Help & feedback

There are a few options here, but the one you want is "Share"; from here you have a few options, but the easiest is to text or email the contact to your friend. This sends them a contact card. So if you have other information with that contact (such as email) then that will be sent over as well.

Delete Contact

There are a few more options on that menu I just showed. If you decide a person is dead to you and you never want to contact them again, then you can return to that menu and tap "Delete." This erases them from your phone, but not your life.

Get Organized

Once you start getting lots of contacts, then it's going to make finding someone more time-consuming. Labels helps. You can add a label for "Family" for instance, and then stick all of your family members there.

When you open your contacts and tap those three lines in the upper left corner, you'll see a menu. This is where you'll see your labels. So with labels, you can jump right into that list and find the contact you need.

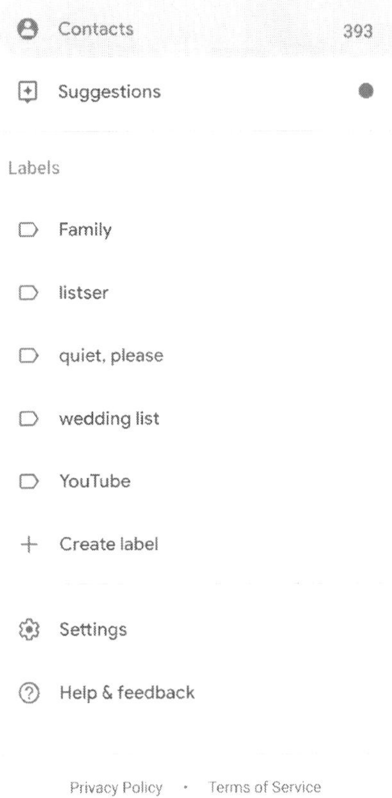

You can also send the entire group inside the label an email or text message. So for instance, if your child is turning 2 and you want to remind everyone in your "Family" contact not to come, then just tap on that label, and then tap on the three dots in the upper right corner. This brings up a menu of options.

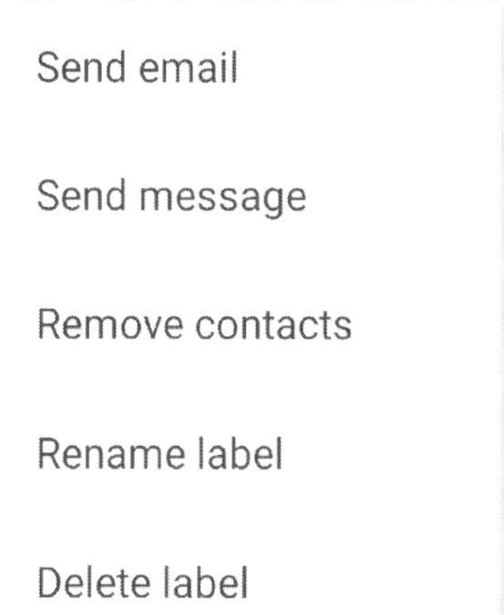

From here, just tap send email or send message.

But what if you don't have labels? Or if you want to add people to a label? Easy. Remember that long application you used to add a contact? One of the fields was called "Labels." You have to tap more to see it. It's all the way at the bottom. One of the last fields, in fact.

If you've never added a label or want to add a new one, then just start typing. If you have another one that you'd like to use, then just tap the arrow and select it.

When you are done, don't forget to tap "Save."

Delete Label

If you decide you no longer want to have a label, then just go to the menu I showed you above—side menu, then the three dots. From here, tap the "Delete Label."

If there's just one person you want to boot from the label, then tap them and go to the label and delete it.

Making Calls

That concludes our sidetrack into the Contacts app. We can now return to getting back to making phone calls to the Ghostbusters.

You can make a call by opening the Contacts app, then selecting the contact, and then tapping on their phone number. Alternatively, you can tap on the Phone button from your Home screen or favorite bar.

There are a few options when you open this app. Let's talk about each one.

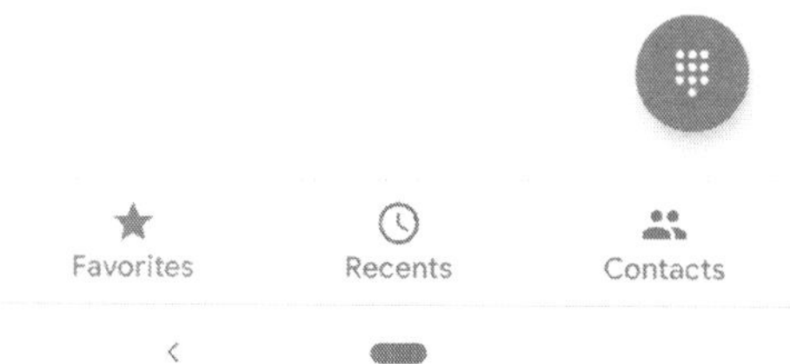

Starting from the far left is the Favorites tab. If you tap this, then you'll see your favorite contacts. If you haven't added any, then this will be empty. If you want to make someone your favorite, then tap them in your Contacts, and tap the star on the top by their name. Once you do that, they'll automatically start showing up here.

In the middle is the Recents tab. If you've made any calls, they'll show here.

The last option is Contacts, which opens a version of the Contacts app that's within the Phone app.

Also on the right is the dial button.

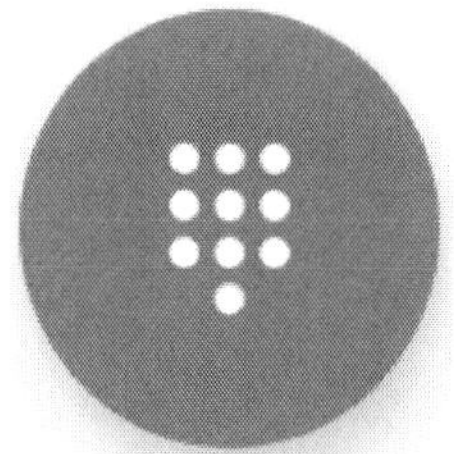

If you want to dial someone the old-fashioned way by tapping in numbers, then tap this.

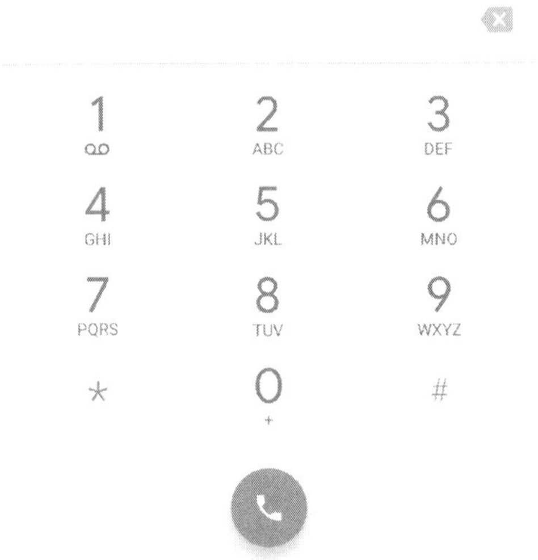

When you are done with the call, hit the "End" button on your phone.

Answer and Decline Calls

What do you do when someone calls you? Probably ignore it because it's a telemarketer!

It's easy to accept a call, however. When the phone rings, the number will appear and if the person is in your Contacts, then the name will appear as well. To answer, just swipe the "answer." To decline just drag the "decline."

Play Angry Birds While Talking to Angry Mom

What if you're on a call with your mom and she's just complaining about something, but you don't want to be rude and hang up? Easy. You multitask! This means you could play Angry Birds while talking!

To multitask, just swipe up from the bottom of your phone, and open the app you want to work in while you are talking. The call will show in the notification area. Tap it to return to the call.

DIRECT MY CALL

Direct My Call came out in 2021 as a way to help you quickly navigate automated menus. The AI on the Pixel 7 is able to detect the menus and put a call menu on your screen, which makes it easier to get where you want to go before the voice on the line says it. It's a feature that will improve over time, so it may not work as expected at first.

To use it, open the Phone app, then tap the three-dot menu icon in the upper corner and select "Settings." Go to "Direct My Call" then toggle it on.

HOLD FOR ME

Google Assistant has become quite literally, your assistant. This is especially true on phone calls. Have you ever been on hold for way too long? Google Assistant knows your pain and is willing to hold for you! It will tell you when it detects a human has picked up. To use it, open the Phone app, tap the three-dot menu in the upper-right corner and select "Settings." Last, tap "Hold for Me."

DON'T BE SPAMMY

Nobody likes that call asking if you want to buy something. Google can help filter your calls and get rid of spam. To turn it on go to the Phone app, then tap those three dots in the upper right corner, and tap settings. Go to "Spam and Call Screen." Tap the toggle next to "See caller and spam ID".

MESSAGES

Now that you know how Contacts and Phone works, messaging will be like second nature. They share many of the same properties.

Let's open up the Messages app (it's on your Favorites bar).

CREATE / SEND A MESSAGE

When you have selected the contact(s) to send a message to, tap Compose. You can also manually type in the number in the text field.

You can add more than one contact--this is known as a group text.

Use the text field to type out your message. If you want to add anything fancy to your message (like photos or gifs) then tap the plus sign. This brings up a menu with more options.

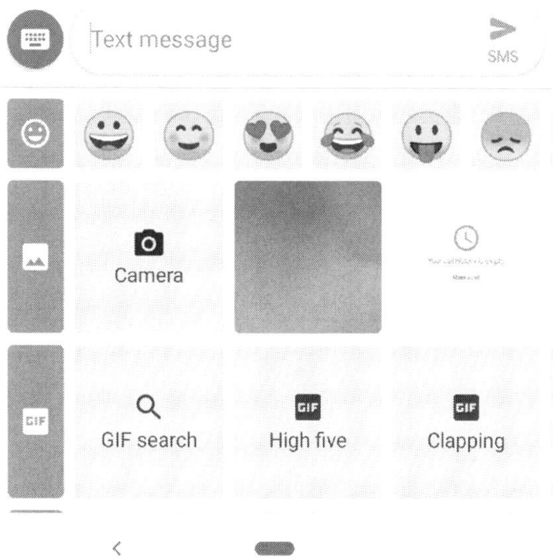

When you are ready to send your message, tap the arrow with the SMS under it.

View Message

When you get a message, your phone will vibrate, chirp, or do nothing—it all depends on how you set up your phone. To view the message, you can either open the app, or swipe down to see your notifications—one will be the text message.

Conversations

Google took big strides in Android 11 to make replying to messages more streamlined and effortless.

One place you see this is with Conversations. When you get a message (text, Facebook message, Twitter message, etc), you'll see that in your notification area by swiping down from the top.

The old method was to click that message to reply. Now you can see the message, set the priority level, and reply right from this area.

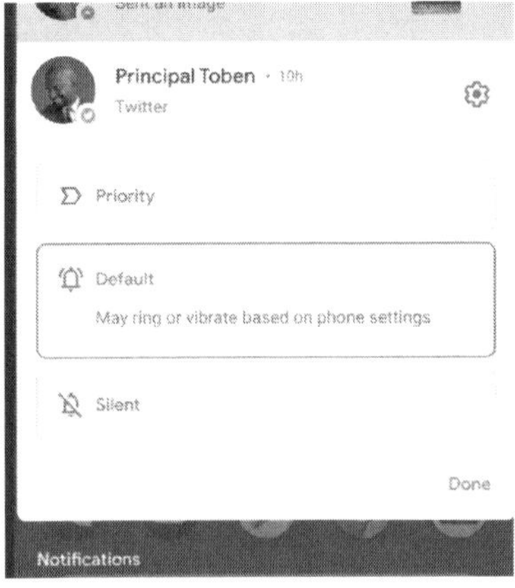

Chat Bubbles

Another area you'll see Android 11 streamline approach to messages is with Chat Bubbles. Chat Bubbles will appear on the side of whatever app you are working in, so you can reply without actually closing the app. As the name suggests, they'll be little bubbles on the side of your screen.

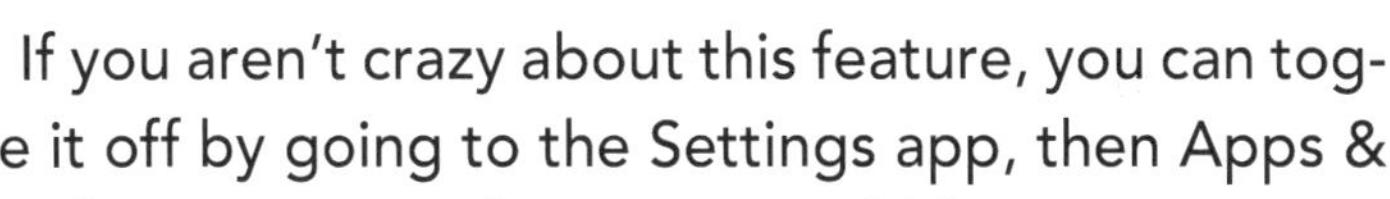

If you aren't crazy about this feature, you can toggle it off by going to the Settings app, then Apps & Notifications> Notifications > Bubbles.

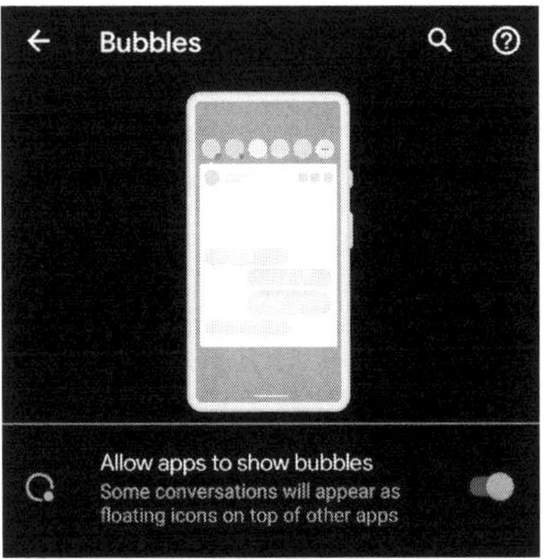

Smart Reply

If you're a Gmail user, you've probably started to see Smart Replies in your email. Smart Reply uses a computer engine to recognize what you will type next and make a suggestion.

Smart Reply works so surprisingly well you might be a little creeped out by it—like it will feel like some person is on the other end of the screen reading your messages! That's not the case. It's all artificial intelligence. But if you still find the feature either creepy or annoying then you can go to the Settings app, then search for Smart Reply. Under Suggestions in chat, you'll see a on / off toggle for the feature.

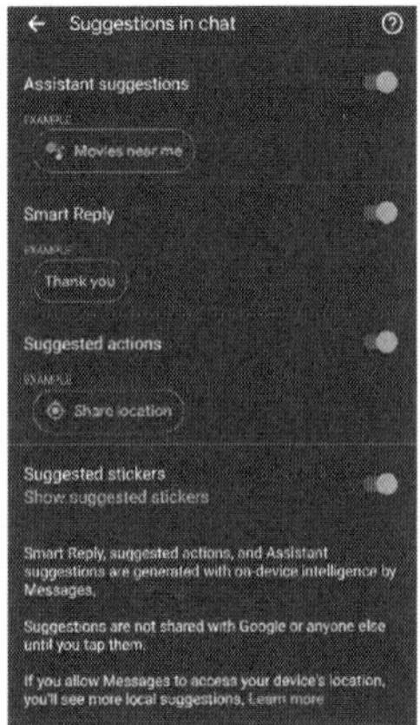

WHERE'S AN APP FOR THAT?

I mentioned earlier that you could play Angry Birds while talking to your angry mom on the phone. Sound fun? But where is Angry Birds on your phone? It's not! You have to download it.

Adding and removing apps on the Pixel is easy. Head to your favorite bar on the bottom of your Home screen and tap the Google Play app.

This launches the Play Store.

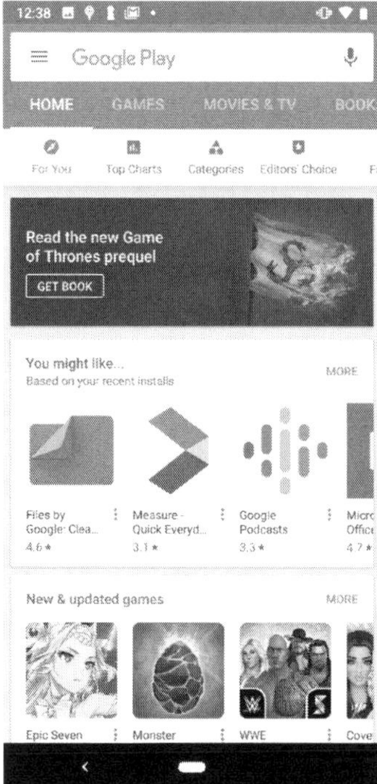

From here you can browse the top apps, see editors' picks, look through categories, or, if you have an app in mind, search for it. The Play Store isn't just for apps. You can use the tabs on the top to go to movies, books, and music. Any kind of downloadable content that's offered by Google can be found here.

When you see the app you want, tap on it. You can read through reviews, see screenshots, and install it on your phone. To install, simply tap the install button—if it's a paid app you'll be prompted to buy it. If there's no price, it's free (or offers in-app payments—which means the app is free, but there are premium features inside it you may have to pay for).

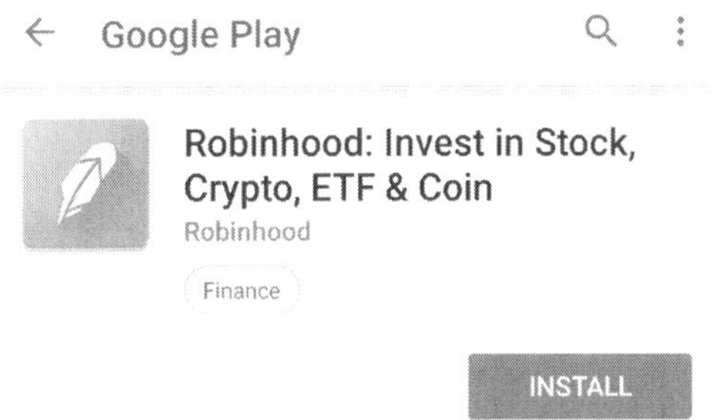

The app is now stored in the app section of your device (remember the section you get to when you swipe up from the bottom to the top?).

Remove App

If you decide you no longer want an app, go to the app in the app menu and tap and hold it. This brings up a box that says "App info." Tap that.

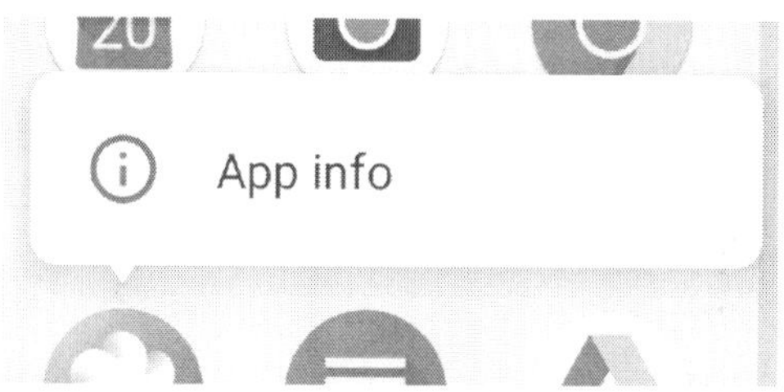

From this menu, you'll get all the information about the app; one of the options is to remove it. Tap that and you're done.

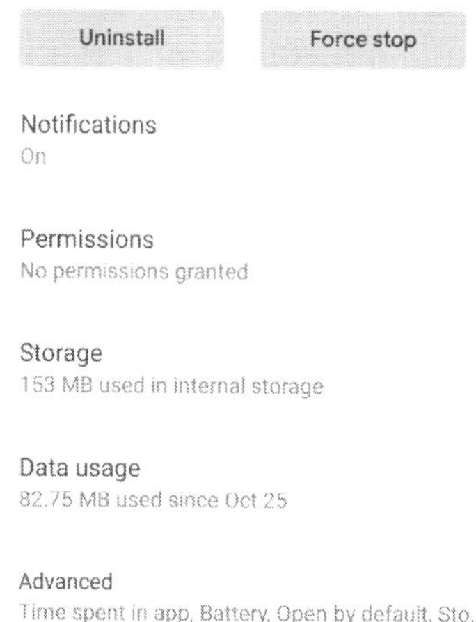

If you download the app from the Play Store, you can always delete it. Some apps that were pre-installed on your phone cannot be deleted.

DRIVING DIRECTIONS

Back in the day, you may have had a GPS. It was a fancy plastic device that would give you directions for anywhere in North America. You can throw out that device because your phone is your new GPS.

To get directions, swipe up to open up your apps. Tap the Maps app.

It's automatically going to be set to wherever you are currently at—which is both creepy and useful.

To get started, just type where you want to go. I'm searching for an amusement park in Anaheim.

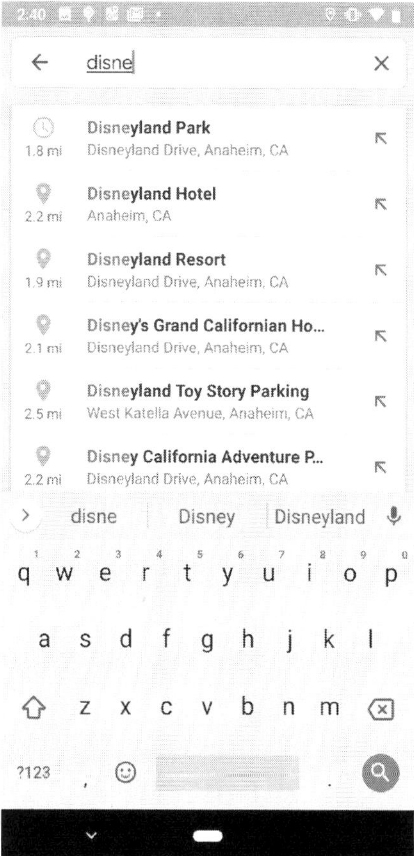

It automatically starts filling in what it thinks you are going to type and tells you the distance. When you see the one you want, tap it.

It pinpoints the location on the map and also gives you an option to call, share or get directions to the location. If you want to zoom out or in, just use two fingers and pinch in or out on the screen.

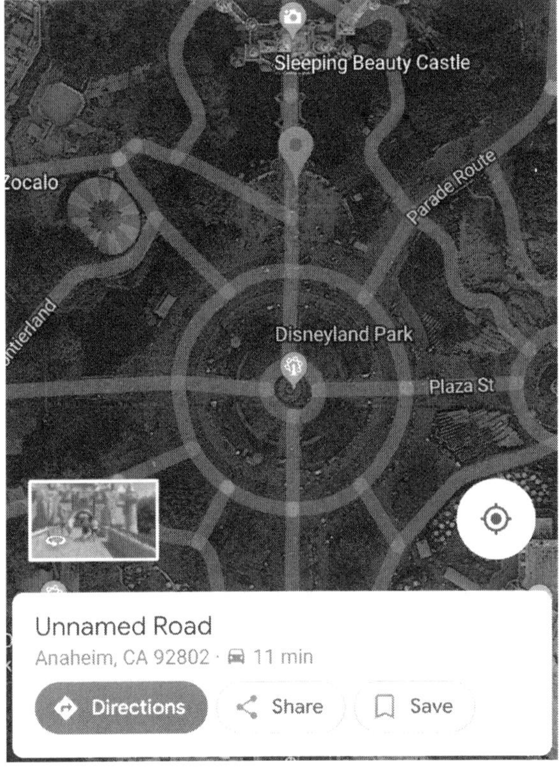

It automatically gets directions from where you are. Want it from a different location? Just tap on the "Your location" field and type where you want to go. You can also reverse the directions by tapping on the double arrows. When you are ready to go, tap "Start."

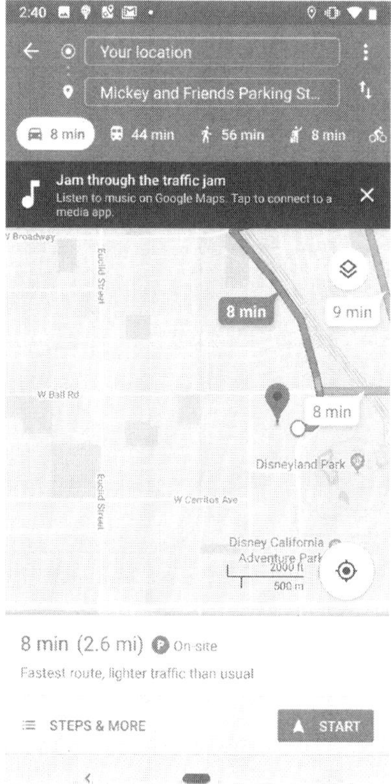

What if you don't want to drive? What if you want to walk? Or bike? Or take a taxi? There are options for all of those and more! Tap the slider under the address bar to whatever you prefer. This updates the directions—when you walk, for example, it will show you one-way streets and also update the time it will take you.

What if you want to drive but are like me: terrified of freeways in California? There's an option to avoid highways. Tap the menu button in the upper right corner of the screen, then select what you want to avoid, and hit "done." You are now rerouted to a longer route—notice how the times probably changed?

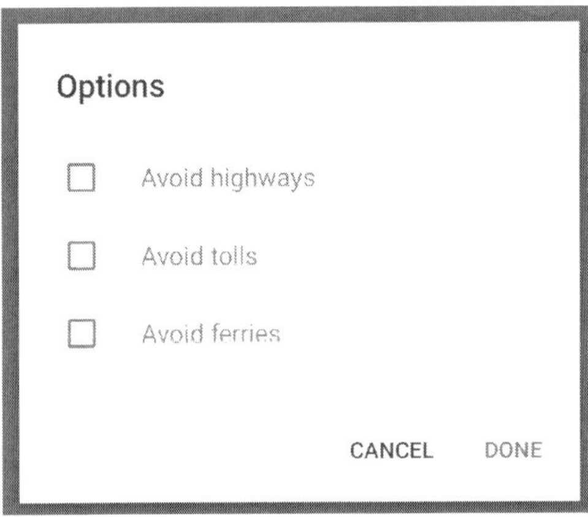

Once you get your directions, you can swipe up to get turn-by-turn directions. You can even see what it looks like from the street. It's called Street View.

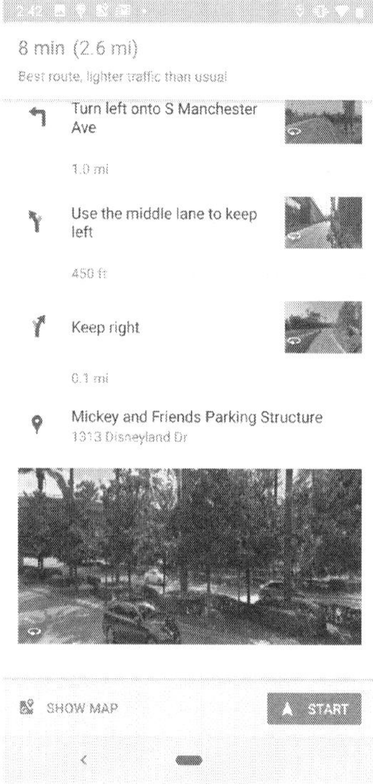

Street View isn't only for streets. Google is expanding the feature everywhere. If you hold your finger over the map, there will be an option to show Street View if it's available. Just tap the thumbnail. Here's a Street View:

You can wander around the entire park! If only you could ride the rides, too! You can get even closer to the action by picking up the Dreamview headset. When you stick your phone in that, you can turn your head and the view turns with you.

Street View is also available in a lot of malls and other tourist attractions. Point your map to the Smithsonian in Washington, DC and get a pretty cool Street View.

WHAT'S THE NAME OF THAT SONG?

We've all had that moment where we are sitting in a coffee shop or standing in an elevator and that "one" song plays. The one we love or hate or just want to know the name to. Yes, there's an app to tell us the name, but sometimes we can't pull it out in time—or we just don't want yet another app on our phone. That's where Now Playing comes in handy.

Now Playing has been around since the Pixel 2, but it often goes unnoticed. It detects music playing around you and adds them to a list that you can look at later. It's all in the background and you don't even know it's running unless you've set up notifications.

To see the songs that have been recorded in your log, go to Settings > Sound > Now Playing. You can see your log by clicking on the history, or you can toggle on the "show songs on lock screen" button.

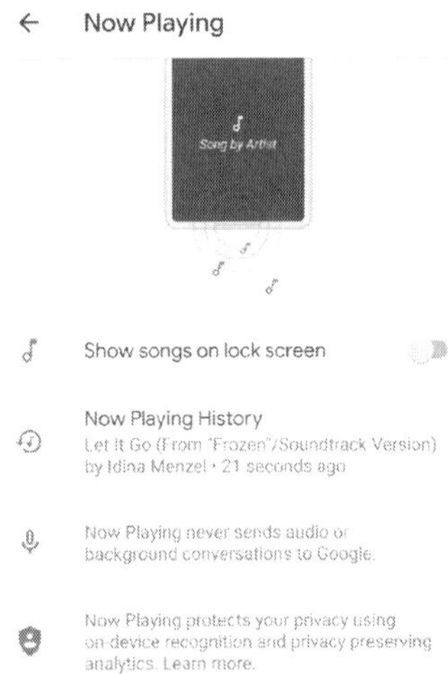

Now Playing
Song by Artist
Show songs on lock screen
Now Playing History
Let It Go (From "Frozen"/Soundtrack Version)
by Idina Menzel • 21 seconds ago
Now Playing never sends audio or
background conversations to Google.
Now Playing protects your privacy using
on-device recognition and privacy preserving
analytics. Learn more.

LIVE CAPTIONING

One of the bigger features to Android 10 is live captioning; live captioning can transcribe any video you record and show what's being said. It works surprisingly well and is pretty accurate.

To turn it on, go to Settings > Sound > Live Caption.

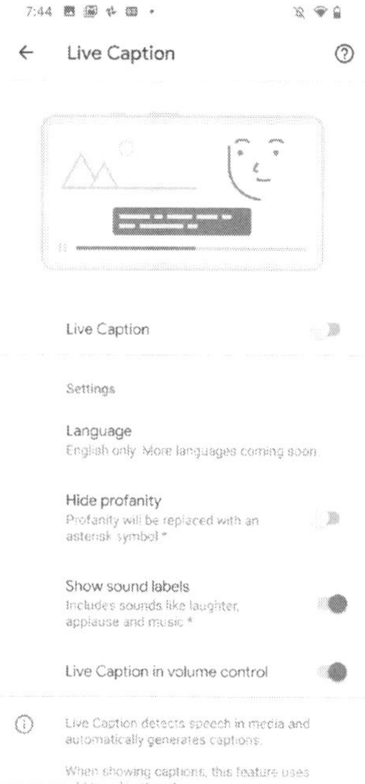

In the settings, you can also toggle off profanity, and, coming soon, select a different language. If it's something you'd only occasionally use, I recommend leaving it toggled off, but having it toggle on under Live Caption in volume control. With that toggled on, all you have to do is press the volume button. Once you do that, you'll see the option to turn it on; it's the bottom option.

Once it's on, you'll start seeing a transcription appear in seconds.

REFRESH RATE

The Pixel 5 supports up to 90Hz refresh rate. Wow, right? Actually, most people have no idea what this means. It's frames per second (FPS)—or 90 FPS. So, what does that mean? If you're playing games or using something that has fast moving action, it means things will seem a lot smoother. It will also eat your battery life to shreds, so use with caution (60Hz is the norm).

To toggle it on / off there are two options. The first way is to go to Settings > Display > Advanced > Smooth Display. This is going to turn it on / off automatically.

If you want to force it on, then there's a second option. Note: this option is "use at your own risk" because it's a developer option. My advice is not to use it unless you know what you are doing. To do it, go to Settings > About phone; go to the very bottom and tap the Build number several times until you are in developer mode. Now go to System > Advanced > Developer Options > Force 90Hz refresh rate.

SHARING WI-FI

Anytime you have guests over, you almost always get the question: what's your wi-fi password. If you are like me, then it probably annoys you. Maybe your password is really long, maybe you just don't like giving out your password, or maybe you are just too embarrassed to say that it's "Feet$FetishLover1." Whatever the reason, then you will love sharing your wi-fi with QR codes. Gone are the days of giving this info out. Just give them a code that they scan, and they'll have access without ever knowing what your password is.

To use it, go to your wi-fi settings, then select the configure button for the wi-fi you want to share.

This will bring up your wi-fI info; tap the blue "Share" option with the QR code.

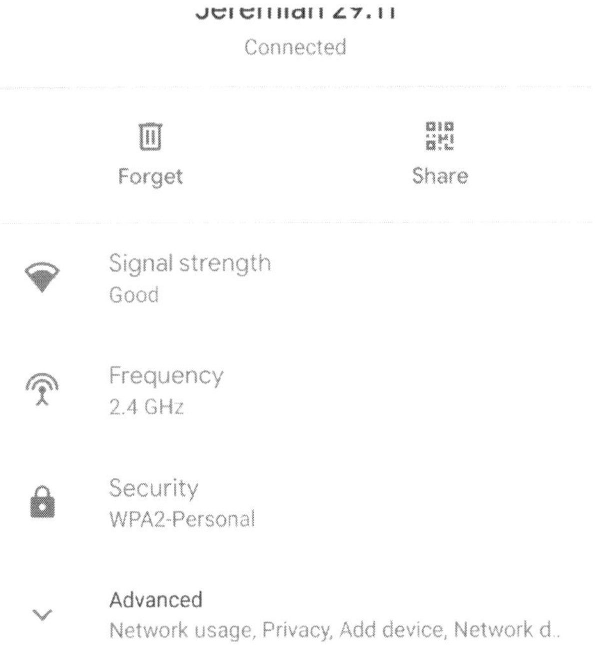

Once you verify that it's you, then you will see the code to scan and you just have to show it to your friend.

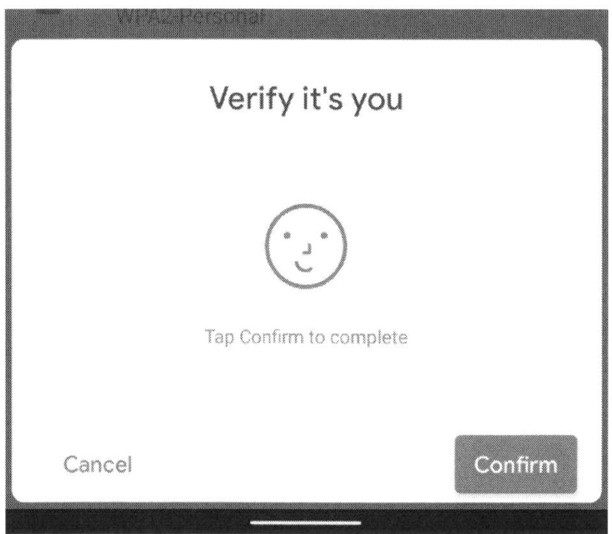

SCREENSHOT

If you've ever run into a problem with your phone and they said, "Take a Screenshot of it" then what they mean on Android is to hold your power button and volume down at the same time. That will screenshot whatever is on your screen and put it in a folder in your photos. Just click library when you open your photo album and you'll see a folder called screenshots.

When you do power + volume down, you'll see a preview appear in your lower left corner. It will disappear in a few seconds, unless you tap that you want to edit it.

If the screen allows it (not all will, so don't get frustrated if you don't see this option at first), you can capture more than what's on your screen; it's called a scrolling screenshot. If available, then you'll see a button that says Capture More. This kind of capture is great for long, text heavy, webpages.

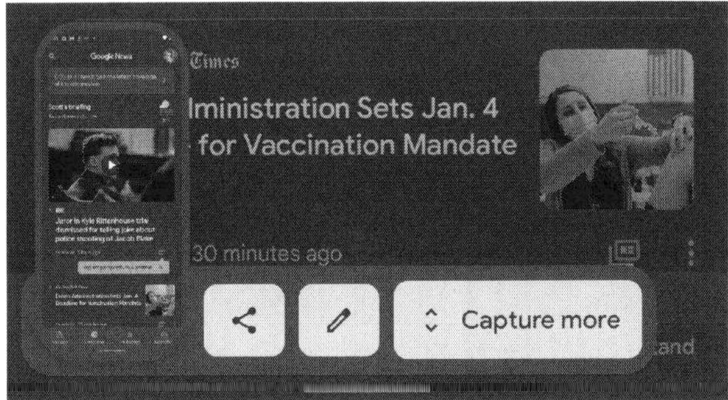

When you tap Capture more, you'll be given the option to drag over the area you want to capture more of. You can do the entire page or just part of it.

GOOGLE RECORDER

Google Recorder has always been a student dream by transcribing what is being recorded automatically. It gets better with the Pixel 7 (though the feature was not available at this writing) by letting you label who's speaking; if, for example, you have an interview with several people, it will detect who is saying what.

00:06
Hello. This is a test.
English (US)
Audio
Transcript
00:14.9
Delete
Save

[5]

LET'S GO SURFING NOW!

This chapter will cover:

- Setting up email
- Creating and sending email
- Managing multiple accounts
- Browsing the Internet

When it comes to the Internet, there are two things you'll want to do:

- Send email
- Browse the Internet

ADD AN EMAIL ACCOUNT

When you set up your phone, you'll set it up to your Google Account, which is usually your email.

You may, however, want to add another email account—or remove the one you set up.

To add an email, swipe up to bring up your apps, and tap on "Settings."

Next, tap on "Accounts."

From here, select "Add Account"; you can also tap on the account that's been set up and tap remove account—but remember you can have more than one account on your phone.

Once you add your email, you'll be asked what type of email it is. Follow the steps after you select the email type to add in your email, password, and other required fields.

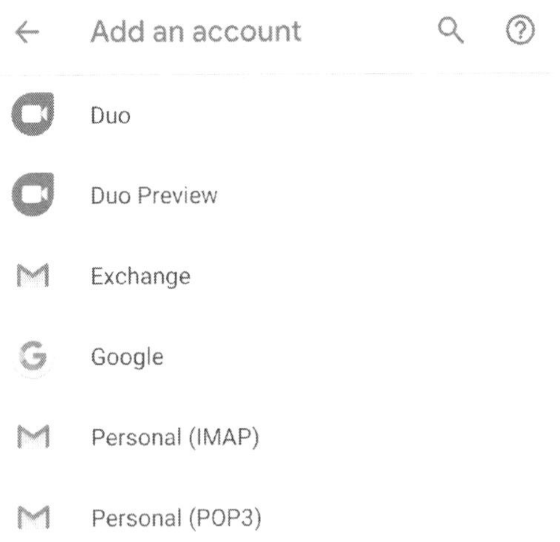

CREATE AND SEND AN EMAIL

To send an email using Gmail (Pixel's native email app), swipe up to get to your apps, tap "Gmail," and tap "Compose a New Email" (the little round red pencil in the lower right corner). When you're done, tap the send button.

You can also use the Google Play Store to find other email apps (such as Outlook).

MANAGE MULTIPLE EMAIL ACCOUNTS

If you have more than one Gmail account, tap the three lines at the upper left of your email screen; this brings out a slider menu. If you tap on the little arrow next to the email address, it drops down and will show other accounts. If none are listed, you can add one.

SURFING THE INTERNET

Google's native Web browser is Chrome. You can use other browsers (which can be found in the Google Play Store). This book will only cover Chrome, however.

Get started by tapping on the Chrome browser icon from your favorite bar, or by going into all programs.

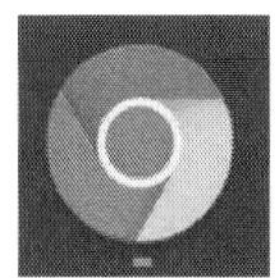

If you've used Chrome on a desktop or any other device, then this chapter won't exactly be rocket science—just like the email app, many of the same properties you find on the desktop exist on the mobile version.

When you open it, you'll see it's a pretty basic browser. There are three main things that you'll want to note.

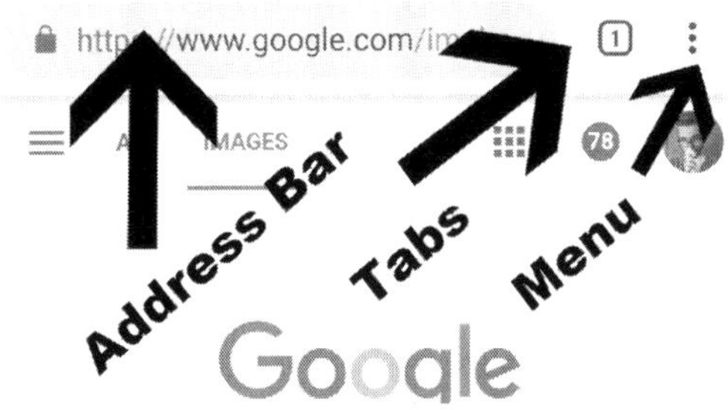

- **Address Bar** - As you would guess, this is where you put the Internet address you want to go to (google.com, for example); what you should understand, however is that this is not just an address bar. This is a search bar. You can use it to search for things just as you would searching for something on Google; when you hit the enter key, it takes you to the Google search results page.

- **Tab Button** - Because you are limited in space, you don't actually see all your tabs like you would on a normal browser; instead you get a button that tells you how many tabs are open. If you tap it, you can either toggle between the tabs, or swipe over one of the pages to close the tab.

- **Menu Button** - The last button brings up a menu with a series of other options that I'll talk about next.

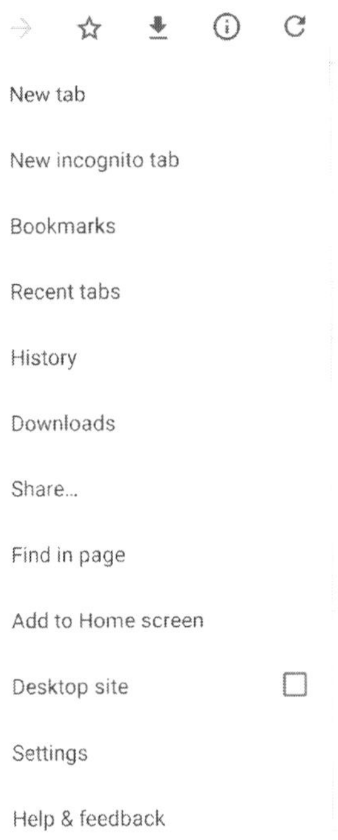

New tab
New incognito tab
Bookmarks
Recent tabs
History
Downloads
Share...
Find in page
Add to Home screen
Desktop site
Settings
Help & feedback

The menu is pretty straightforward, but there are a few things worth noting.

"New incognito tab" opens your phone into private browsing; that doesn't mean your IP isn't tracked. It means your history isn't record; it also means passwords and cookies aren't stored.

A little bit further down is "History"; if you want your history erased so there's no record on your phone of where you went, then go here, and clear your browsing history.

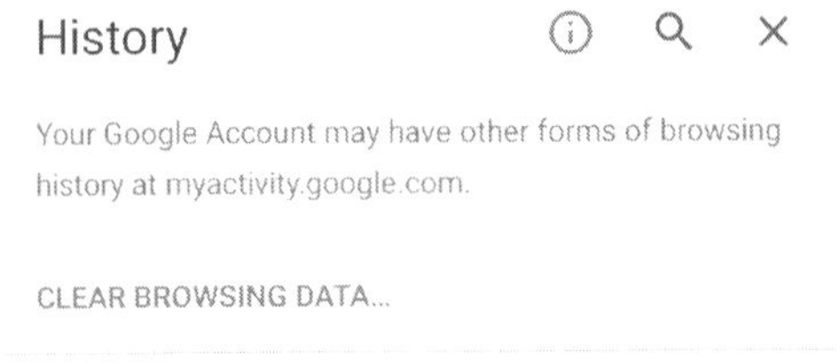

History

Your Google Account may have other forms of browsing history at myactivity.google.com.

CLEAR BROWSING DATA...

If you want to erase more than just websites (passwords, for example) then go to "Settings" at the very bottom of the menu. This opens up more advance settings.

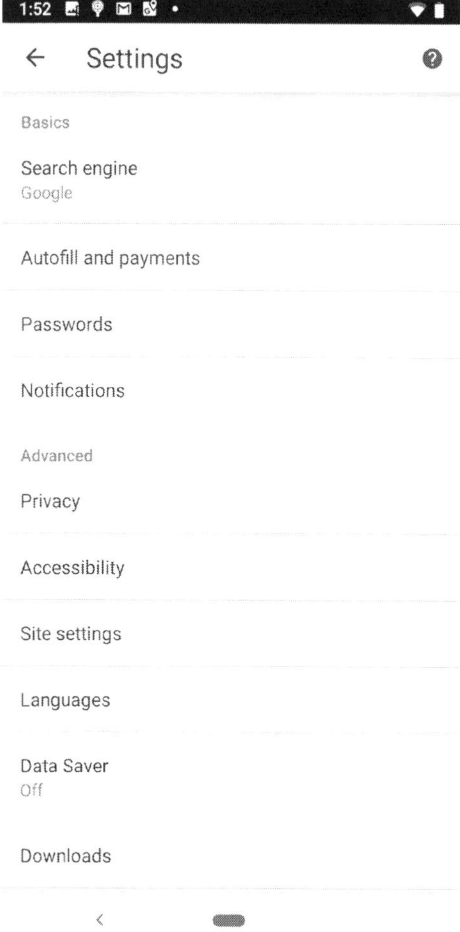

[6]

SNAP IT!

This chapter will cover:

- How to take different photos
- How to take videos
- Camera settings
- Different camera features

The camera is the bread and butter of the Pixel phone. Many people consider the Pixel to be the greatest camera ever on a phone. I'll leave that for you to decide.

One of the nice things about photos on the Pixel is it stores them online automatically, so you don't have to worry about losing them. You can see them by logging into the Google account associated with your Pixel and going here:

https://photos.google.com

Best of all: this is all free! You don't have to pay extra for more storage and it doesn't go against other things in your Google Drive.

To make sure you have this feature on, go to "Settings" and "Backup" and "sync"; make sure you toggle it on.

There are some caveats (such as the photos may be compressed), so read the terms.

THE BASICS

Are you ready to get your Ansel Adams on? Let's get started by opening the Camera app. You can do this several ways:

- The most obvious is to tap the Camera on your favorite bar or by swiping up and opening it from all apps. It looks like a camera—go figure!

- Double press the power button.

Once you are in the app, don't forget, you can twist the phone to toggle between selfie mode.

When you open the app, it starts in the basic camera mode. The UI can look pretty simple, but don't be fooled. There are a lot of controls.

The first is at the top. Tap the down arrow at the top of the screen.

The options are pretty straightforward, but "Top Shot" (which used to be called Motion) might be new to you. This is basically like a very short video of your photo. You can turn it on for all photos, auto so it turns on when motion is detected, or turn it off. Top Shot is larger, so storing it in this mode will take a little more space. Night Sight is ideal for when you in low light. The screen below is the basic camera settings, but this menu can differ slightly depending on what camera mode you are in.

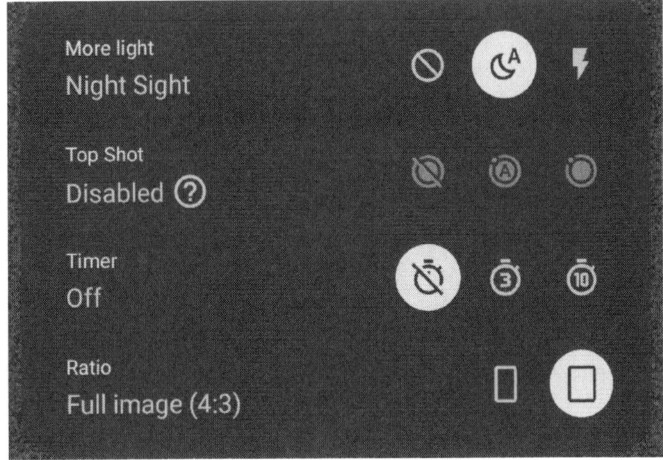

Over on the upper right side is the folder icon; that lets you pick where you will save the photo you are currently shooting.

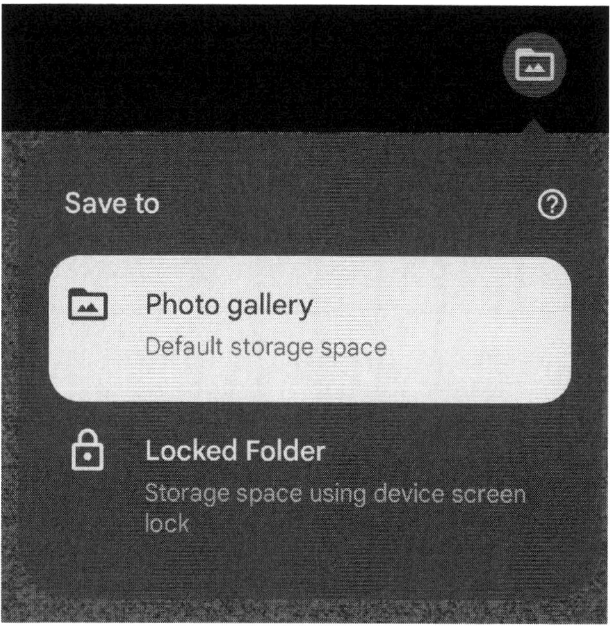

On the bottom of the screen are all the modes and the shutter. Starting with the top row from the left you have the selfie button, the shutter, and the last photo preview (tapping that will show all of your photos that you have taken starting with the most recent). On the bottom, you have the camera modes, which I'll cover in more detail later in this chapter.

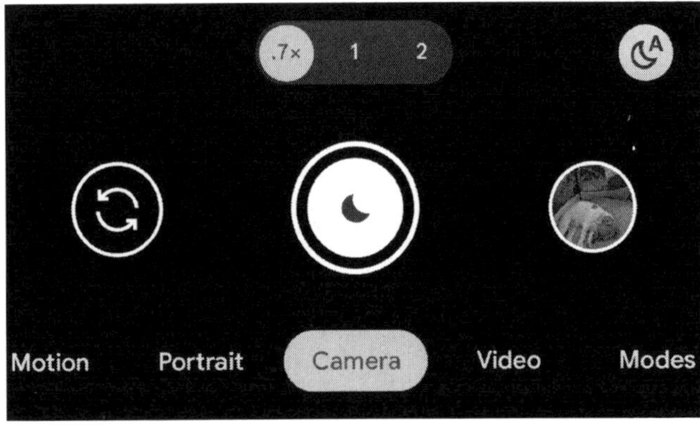

When you point your camera at a product and tap and hold over that product, this will activate Google Lens, which will try to detect what you are pointing at and give you more information about it. It's not always 100% accurate (for example, I pointed it at the Pixel 5 case and it showed me info for the Pixel 3), but it's still a nice feature.

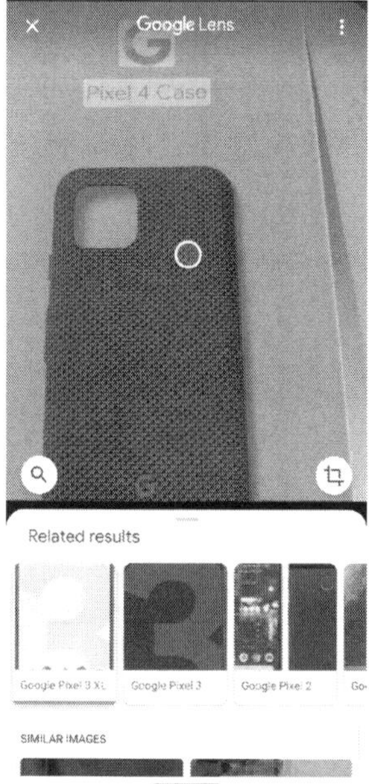

If you tap once, but don't hold, this will bring up exposure and zoom options (you can also pinch in and out to zoom). Tapping on the area of the screen that you want to focus on will also focus on that area; for example, if you point it at a group of people in front of a crowd of people, you can tap the group to tell the camera that's the focus of the show.

When you tap in the middle of the screen as you prepare to take a shot, you can use the sliders to control the amount of brightness, contrast or warmth the photo has.

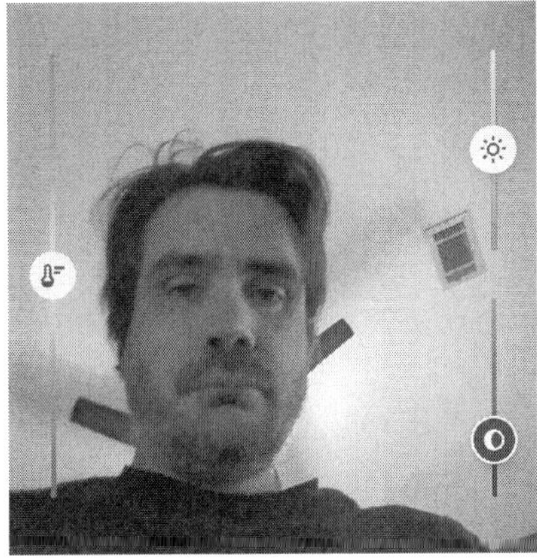

One final thing I will point out about taking pictures. Remember up in the top bar (when you swipe down), there's an option to disable the camera or mic? Well you sort of need those things to take photos and videos, right? If you try and do it when they're on, you'll get the message below. Tap the unlock button to enable the features.

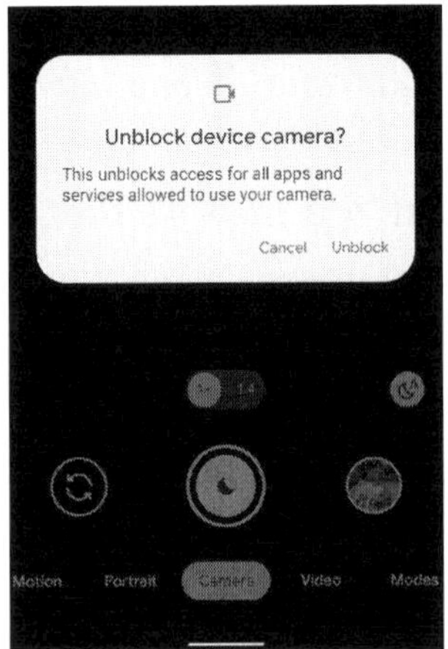

HELLO (PHOTO) FRIEND

Do you have people you take photos of more than others? A kid? A partner? A friend? A pet? Google's AI can prioritize people you photograph most. To turn it on go to the Camera app, open the settings and enable Frequent Faces.

CAMERA MODES

Let's look at each of the modes next.

Think of modes like different lenses. You have your basic camera lens, but then you can also have a lens for fisheye, and close up. If you look at the bottom of your camera app, you can slide left and right to get to the different modes. In 2019, Google added Night Sight mode, which helps you capture better photos at night. It works like the basic Camera mode. It also turns on automatically when it detects you are shooting in night.

Next to Night Sight is Portrait mode. Portrait mode gives your photos a sharp professional look to them. It blurs the background to really make your photos pop. I'll show an example with a photo of myself—apologies in advance for my looks!

Here I am with zero blur:

And here I am with maximum blur:

So how do you do that? First, slide to the Portrait mode. The phone will try to figure out where the focal point will be, but you'll get the best effect if you tap on the screen where the focus will be. If you tap on the face, for example, it will tell the phone you want to blur everything else. The change won't be noticeable—you can edit it after.

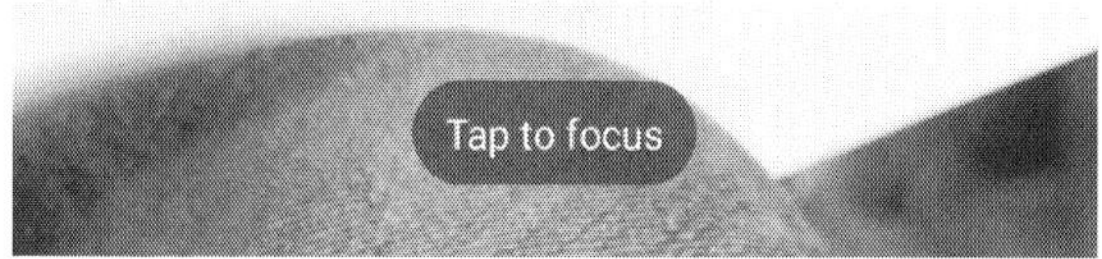

I'll show you how to edit that blur a little later in this section.

Video mode takes, you guessed it, videos! Once you tap record, there are not as many settings as the camera. To the left, there's a pause button, the middle is the stop button, and the far right is the camera shutter—that means as you are recording you can still take photos.

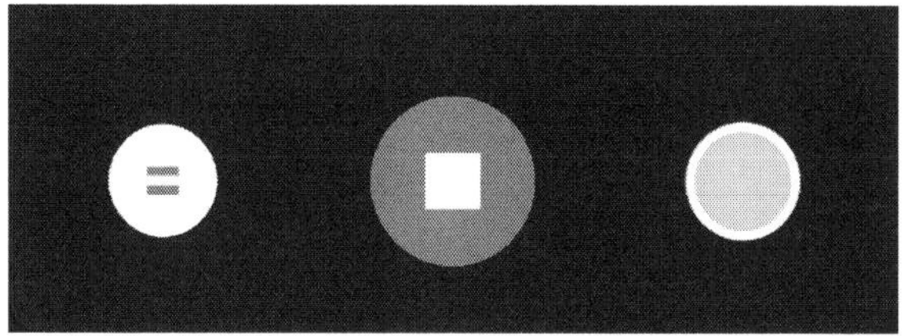

When you tap to focus on a subject, you'll notice that there's only a slider for zoom (bottom), and brightness (right side); there's also a lock to lock in on your focus.

There's also a Cinematic video mode that takes videos with the blurred effected—only the main person in the scene is in focus.

Before you shoot a video, there's also an option to toggle between Slow Motion, Normal, and Time Lapse; if you are coming to the Pixel 5 from an earlier model, you'll probably be used to using these modes in another place; they used to be located under "More." Google decided to eliminate that extra step and put all the video modes in one place.

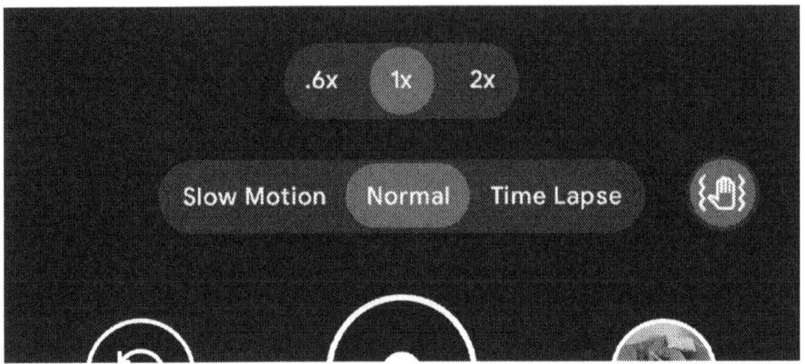

So speaking of this "More" area, let's tap on that next and see the other modes available. There's three more: Panorama, Photo Sphere, and Lens. The modes can take good photos, but they are more fun modes.

Panorama is great for landscape photos. The below photo is an example (note: this was not shot on the Pixel):

The way it works on the Pixel, is you take one photo, and then you move a little to the right and take another, and so on and so forth; then all of those photos are stitched together to make one giant photo. Just hit the arrow button for each photo and the blue button to finish (or X button to cancel).

Photo Sphere is sort of like a panorama photo; it's several photos stitched together. But where a panorama is straight, Photo Sphere is 360 degrees; it's fun for your phone or sharing online (like Facebook). To use it, tap the shutter when in Photo Sphere mode, then move your camera up and down, and left and right.

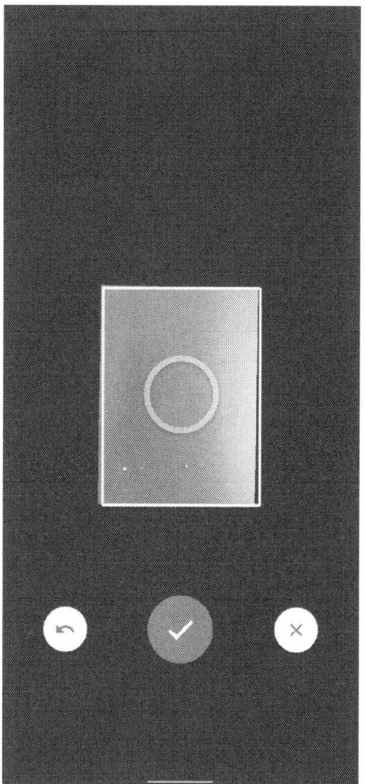

Before you take the photo, you can also tap the down arrow at the top of the screen and change the shape.

When you view the photo, you can either use your finger to move the direction of it, or you can tap the VR mode in the lower right corner and use VR headsets.

The last mode is Lens. I already mentioned how you can activate it in the regular camera mode, but there are more features in the native Lens mode.

You can do automatic, but there are modes within this mode to translate, scan a doc, look for consumer products, or identify food. By default, it's on the automatic mode (the middle one), but tapping on the other icons will switch the mode and give you more accurate results.

Most modes have unique settings. Translate, for example, lets you auto-detect the language you are scanning, or change it to something different.

Depending on what you scan, it will give you information about the product, and you can click for more information.

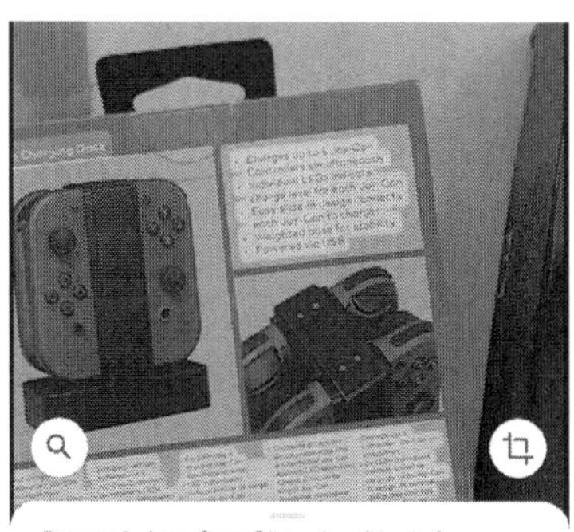

EDITING PHOTO

Once you take a photo, you can begin fine tuning it to really make it sparkle. You can access editing by opening the photo you want to make edits to. This is done by either opening it from the camera app by clicking on the photo preview (next to the shutter);

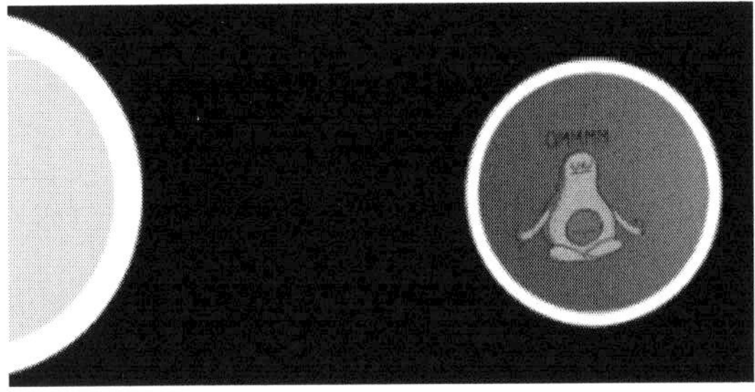

Or by opening the Photo app.

When you open a photo, you'll see either four or five sets of options depending on what kind of photo it is. Portrait photos have more editing options. How do you know what kind of photo it is? The thumbnail will tell you. If you see a timestamp, then it's a video; if there's nothing, then it's a regular photo; if there's a portrait, then it's a Portrait photo; and if there's a moon, then it was taken with Night mode.

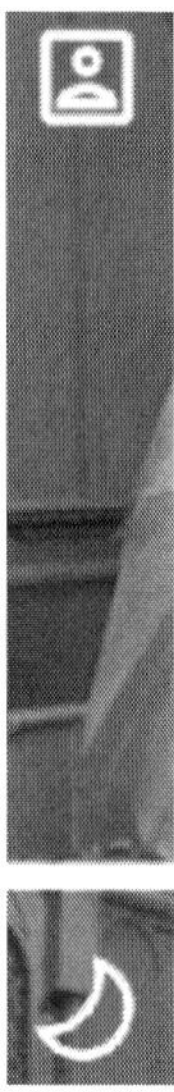

The below are the four options available to all pictures.

And these five options are the ones available to only Portrait photos. Same options, but one additional new one. The middle option is new.

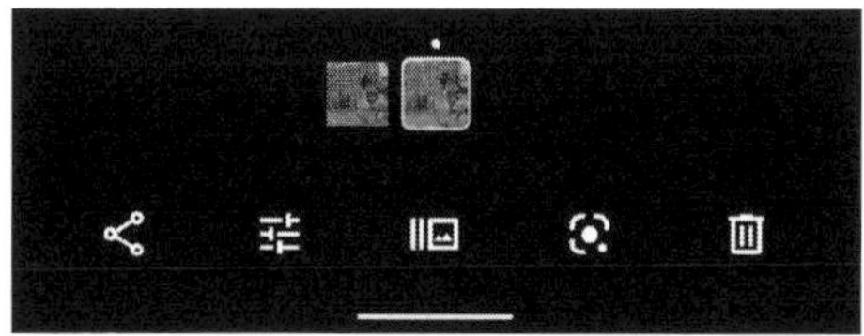

From left to right, the five buttons mean this:

- Share the photo
- Edit the photo
- Keep only one photo (Google takes several shots and will show you the best one)
- Turn on lens
- Delete the photo

The option you want is the second: edit the photo.

Tapping this brings up several powerful options. The first is suggestions. That let's you automatically adjust the photo based on the phones AI's recommendation. Enhance would be the most general one.

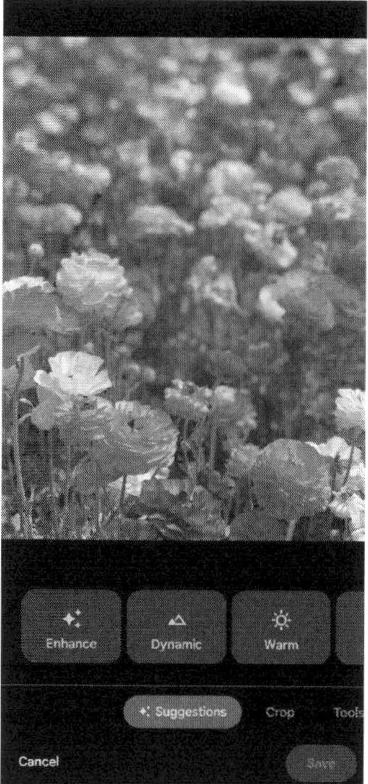

On the bottom of the phone is a slider that lets you see all the other edit options.

The first next to Suggestions is Crop. Don't let the name full you. Yes, you can do the tradition "crop" where you take out some of the photos edges, but this is also where you would go to rotate the photo or change it's direction.

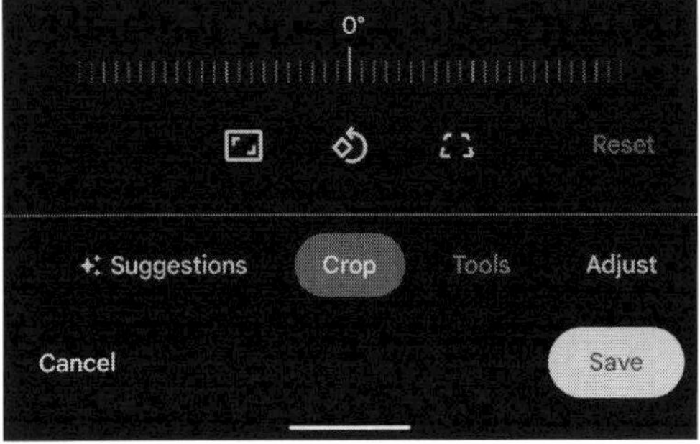

Tools has one of the newest and most exciting features: Magic Erase. Want to erase the photo-bomber from the image? Done! That old high school sweetheart who broke your heart? Gone!

Before talking more about this magic eraser tool, let me briefly mention that if you are editing a portrait photo, you'll see even more options (see image below).

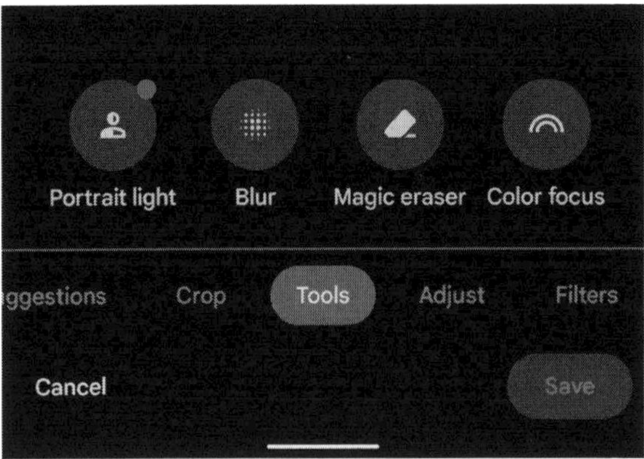

This is where you can change the focus of the image (so you can blur something else), adjust the lighting, or reduce the amount of blur.

But back to that core feature: magic erase. How does it work? Let's take a look. The image below is great, isn't it?! But I don't like that statue on the left.

To remove her, I go into Edit > Tools, select Magic eraser.

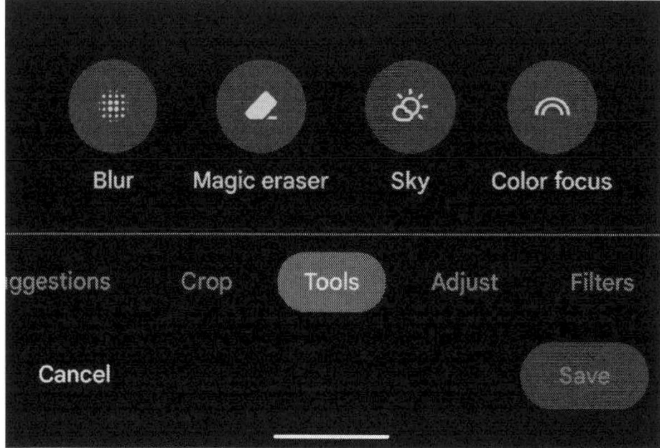

From here, I just rub my finger on the area that I want to erase.

When I'm done, I lift my finger. Poof. She's all gone!

Pretty cool, right? Make sure and tap Done and save it.

If by chance you don't see this feature, then you probably need to update your phone. Also, remember, this feature is currently only available on the Pixel.

Next to Tools is the Adjust button. This is where you can manually adjust things like brightness. Suggestions will also do this, but it will do it automatically.

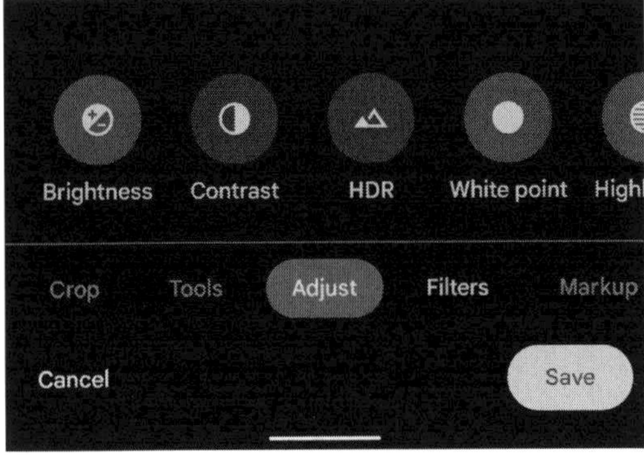

Clicking on any of the settings will bring up a new slighter; move it left or right to adjust the intensity.

Filters is the next setting, and it will automatically apply a filter over the photo. So if you want it to have a Vivid look—i.e. one that's full of bright colors, then tap the Vivid filter.

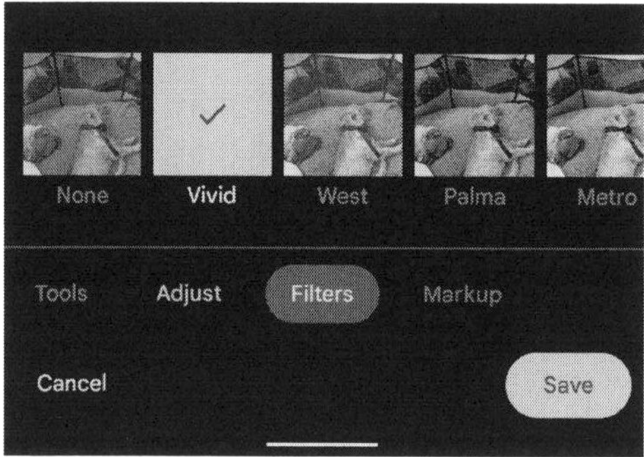

The last setting is Markup. This setting is used to write text or highlight things in the photo. For example, if you want to circle something in the photo that you are trying to point out to someone.

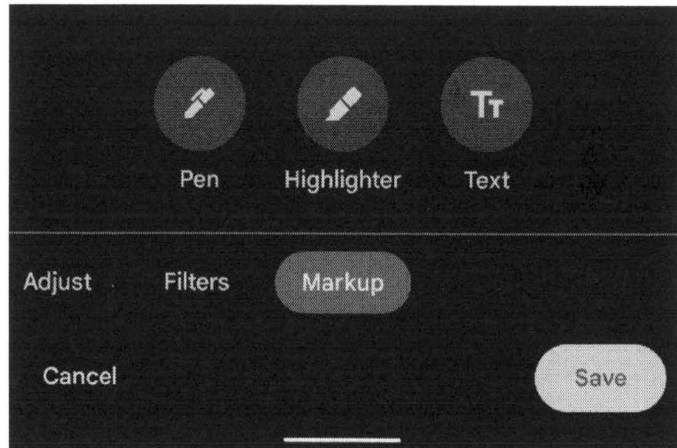

BLURRED PHOTOS

Google's AI really helps photos shine. The unblur feature shows you the full potential of this AI engine; it can take previously blurry photos and sharpen them.

It's under Tools and says Unblur. Tap that once, and it will automatically make the adjustment that it thinks is appropriate for the photo.

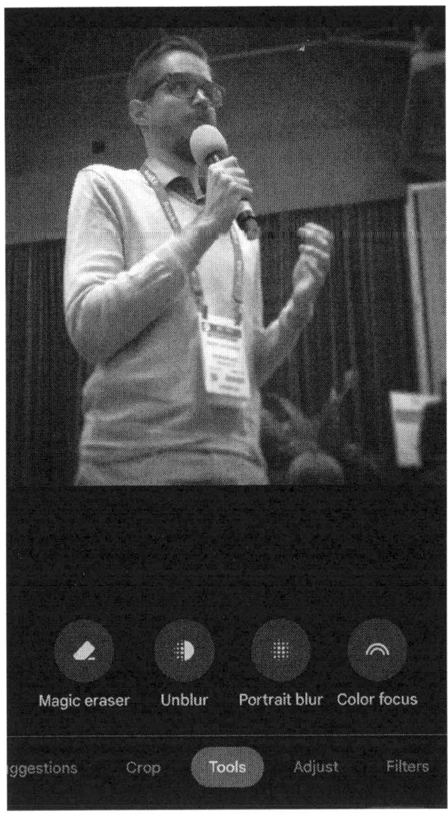

Once the adjustment is made, you'll see a slider that lets you make more adjustments—100 is the max you can go; going down would in values would make the photo more blurry.

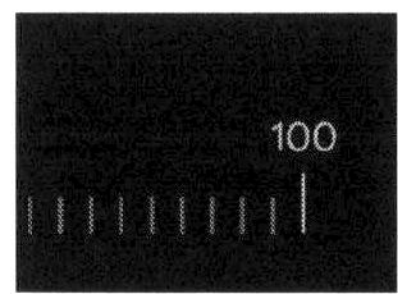

ORGANIZING YOUR PHOTOS

The great thing about mobile photos is you always have a camera ready to capture memorable events; the bad thing about mobile photos is you always have a camera ready to capture events, and you'll find you have hundreds and hundreds of photos very quickly.

Fortunately, Google makes it very simple to organize your photos so you can find what you are looking for.

Let's open up the Photos app and see how to get things organized.

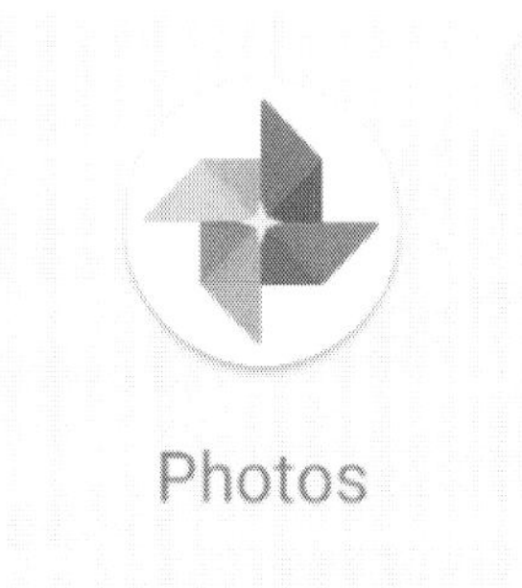

Pixel keeps things pretty simple by having only four options on the bottom of your screen.

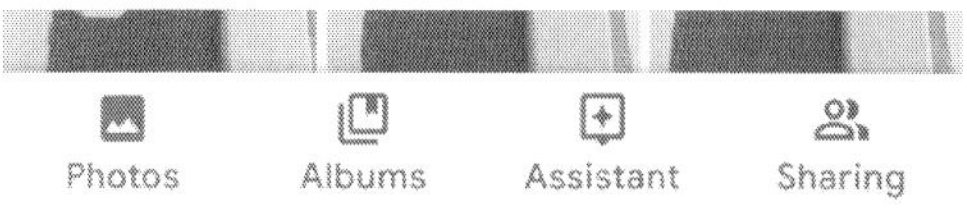

In the upper right corner, there's three dots, which is the photo option menu; that menu is there no matter where you are in the Photo app.

When you tap that menu, you'll get several more options.

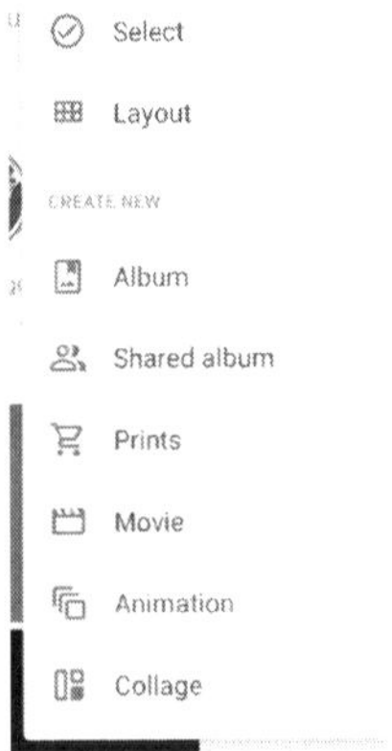

The options are as follows:

- Select – This lets you select photos on your screen so you can share, email, print, and more.
- Layout – There are two Layout modes: Comfortable view (this view creates a grid with small and large photo

thumbnails) and Month view (all thumbnails are the same size.

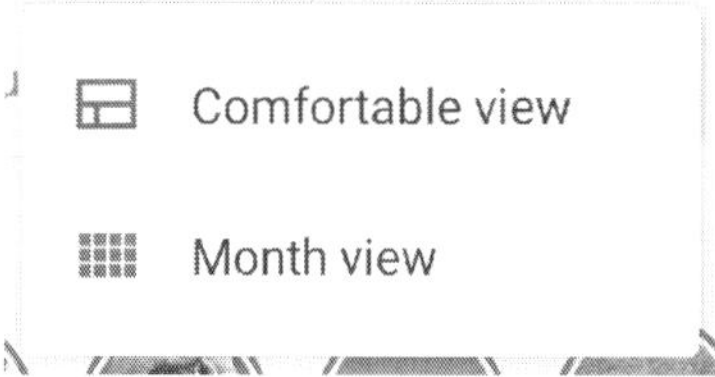

- Album – Let's you create an album by selecting photos or faces.

- Shared album – Lets you share albums.
- Prints – Quickly create photo albums that you can print and have sent to your house.

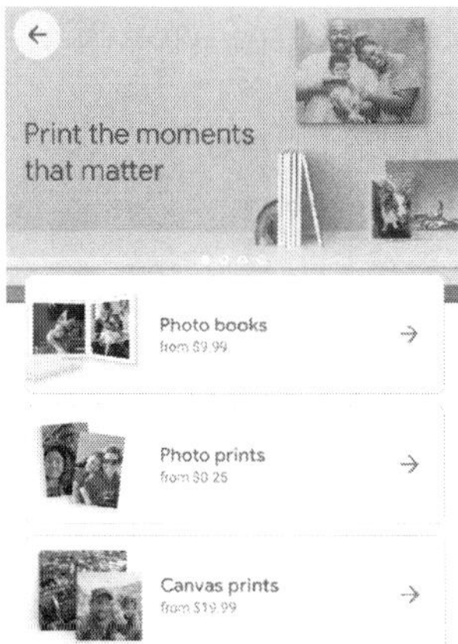

- Movie – Movies lets you create video memories of your photos. You can either select "New movie" and create one based on selected photos or pick from one of the many templates. It can take several minutes for movies to generate when you pick this option.

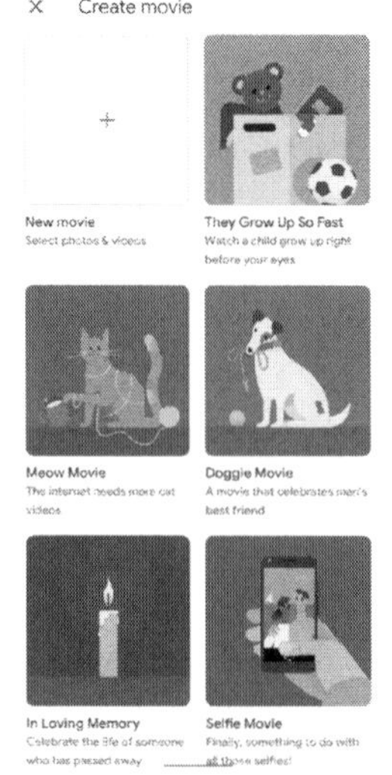

- Animation – Animation is kind of like a .gif; whereas movies could run for several minutes, animations are only a few seconds.
- Collage – Collage lets you pick up to nine photos to combine into one collage. If you pick less, Google will automatically arrange it for you. The below is an example of three photos in a collage. There isn't a lot of customization here, so if you want a collage, you might want to download a free collage app that has a few more tools in it.

In the upper left corner is three lines; this opens your second menu option screen.

Some of the options (such as buy prints) are the same ones you've already seen in the other menu.

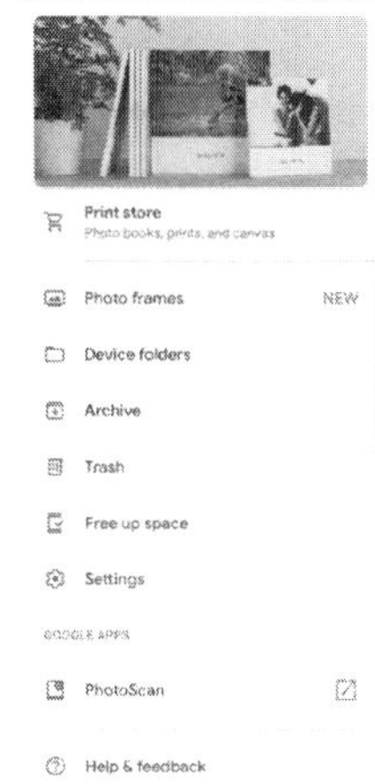

Photo frames is an option available if you have a Google Nest Hub (or Google Hub). This lets you pick the photos that display on your Hub.

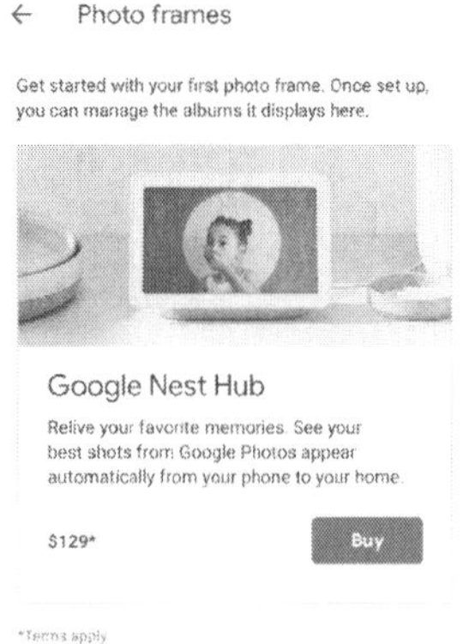

Device folders is where you can find screenshots if you've taken any. You can take a screenshot by pressing the orange button and the down volume button at the same time.

Archive is to help you declutter your phone. You can archive photos so your main photo area has less photos; archiving them puts them here, but they will still be searchable.

Clear the clutter

Archived items will be kept here. They'll still show in albums & search results.

Learn More

If you delete a photo, it is actually not permanently deleted from your device...yet. It is moved here. This is helpful if you have a kid who likes to delete things! If you tap any of the photos, you can restore it or delete it—deleting it means it's gone for good.

"Free up space" removes photos from your device and backs them up to your Google account. You can still view them whenever you want.

Settings will be covered in the next sections.

Finally, PhotoScan is a free app that you have to download to use; the app lets you use your Pixel camera to scan old print photos. It works surprisingly well and is recommended if you have lots of photos that you want saved.

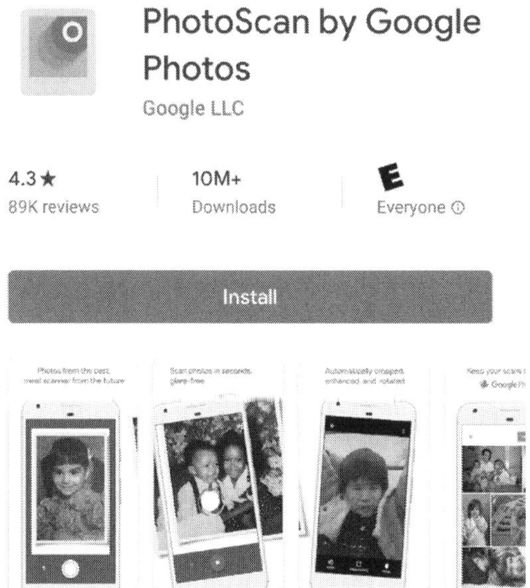

The next tab on the bottom of the Photos app (Albums) is where you can go to start grouping your photos together. There are already things like Places and Things that have albums; if you have starred anything, you'll also see one for Favorites.

What you might not know is Google is quietly working in the background to figure out who is in photos. Once you take several photos, you'll see one called People & Pets.

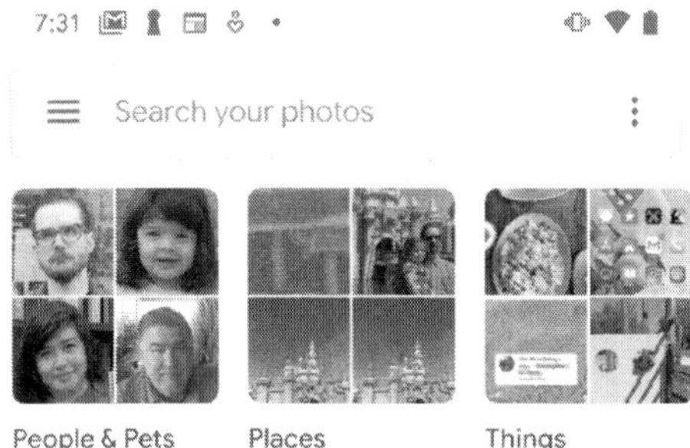

When you open it, you'll see people you probably recognize, and when you click on it, it will show you other photos that they are in. Pretty cool, right? What's cooler is you can name those people, so you can search more easily for them. Just click their face, then tap "Add a name." In the example below, Google has found my dog's face.

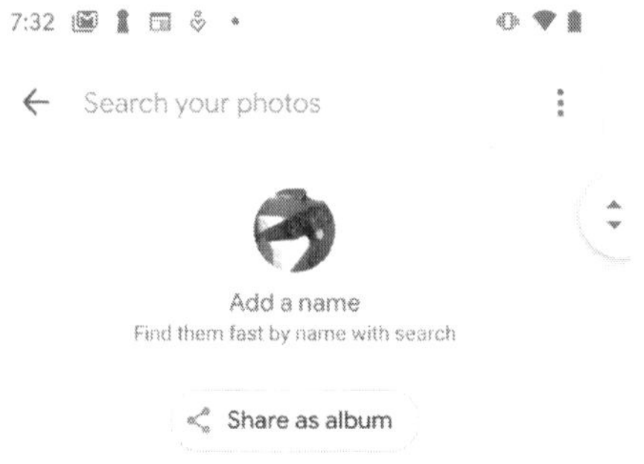

I added her name, so when I go back, I now see her photo with her name. I can now search for photos using her name. You can also search for photos using names of places or even foods or things. The photo search is pretty smart, and it gets even smarter as you take more photos.

When you want to create a new album, just click the three dots in the upper right corner.

It will ask you to name it; you can pick whatever you want. From here, you can either auto select things based on people and pets, or you can select your own photos.

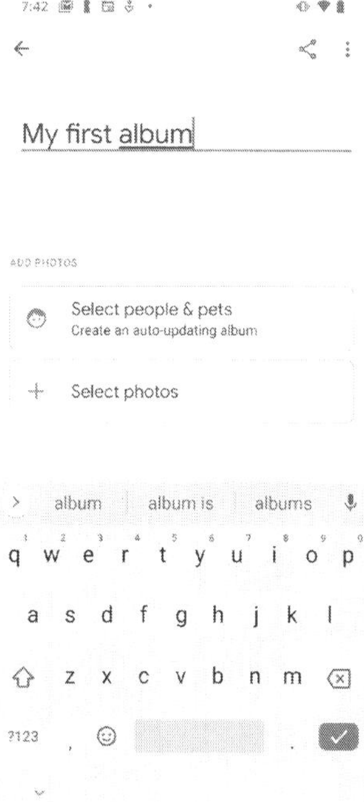

If you select photos on your own, you'll just have to manually tap each one that you want in the album.

If you select to have it auto create, you'll just have to pick what you want to use (a person's name, for example).

Once the album is created, you can tap the three dots in the upper right corner to add more photos, order photos, delete the album, or share.

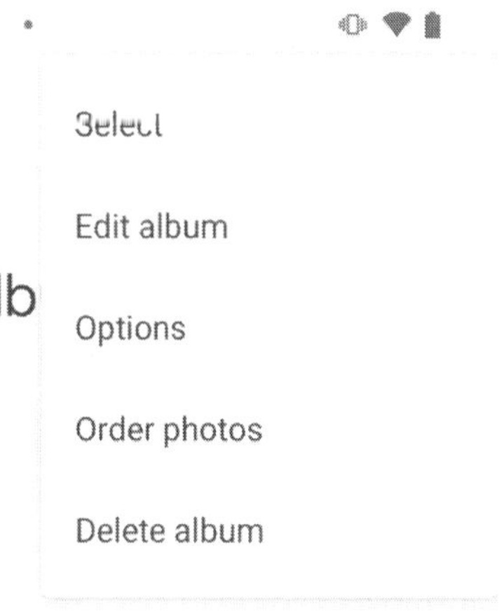

You can also click the Share button on the album (or on any photo), which brings up the Sharing menu. You can share with a link, via email, Bluetooth, text message, and more.

The Assistant option is recommendations from Google's AI bot; it collects memories based on places you've been and groups together what it considers the best shots.

The last option on the bottom menu is Sharing. Sharing lets you select other people who can see your photos. You can, for example, share all photos of a certain person with that person, and you can set it to share new photos of that person whenever you take them.

To get started, just tap the "Add partner account."

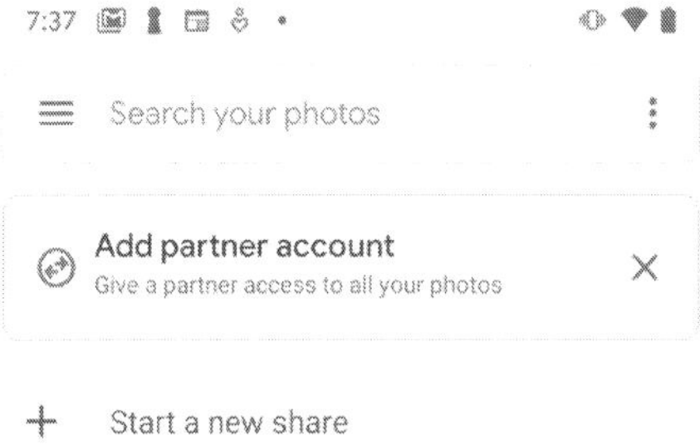

Next you'll see a screen telling you what sharing is. Tap the blue "Get Started" option.

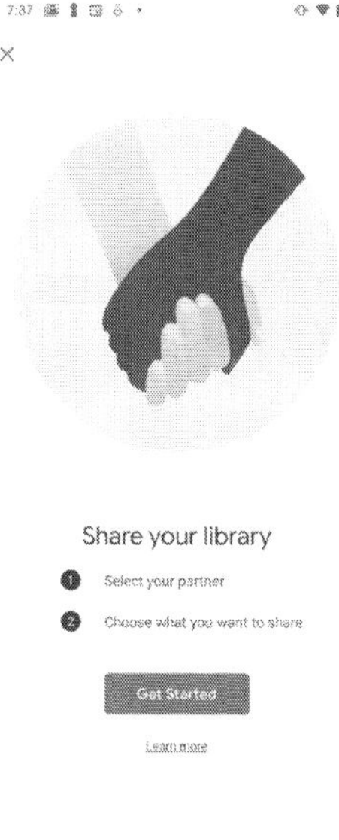

From here you'll search for the person's name or email; Google might also have a few suggested contacts for you, and you can just tap their name.

Once you pick the person, it will ask you what you want to share. You can share every single photo now, and in the future, or you can pick certain people or days.

Choose Settings
Share with diana.lacounte@gmail.com
Next

GRANT ACCESS TO

All photos

Photos of specific people

OLDER PHOTOS

Only show photos since this day
Off

It will confirm what you are sharing before it shares; once you tap "Send invitation," it will email an invite to that person and they have to accept it before they actually see the photos.

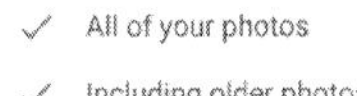

New photos will be shared automatically. Learn more

Send invitation

SETTINGS

You probably won't spend a lot of time in Photo settings, but they're still good to know for those occasions when you do want to make changes.

You can access your settings by opening the Photo app, tapping on the three lines in the upper left corner, then tapping on Settings.

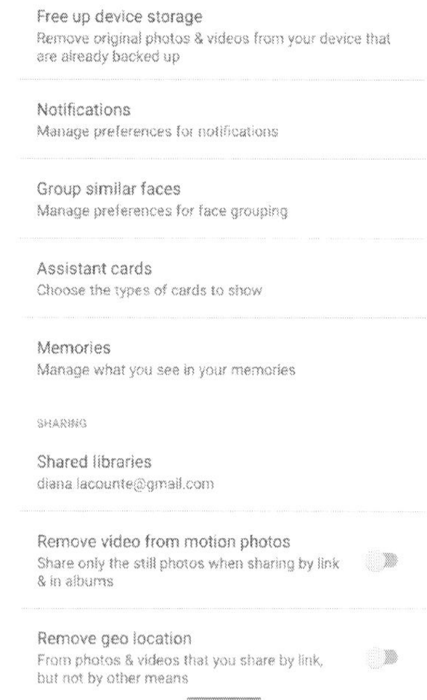

There are three areas of the settings: Main, Sharing, and Google apps.

MAIN SETTINGS

- Back up & sync – Lets you pick how photos are backed up (what email account they are linked to, the resolution of the photos, when to back them up, where to back them up, and more).

- Free up device storage – Removes photos from your device and stores them in your account so you have more room for additional photos.
- Notifications – Lets you pick the kinds of pop up notifications you'll receive regarding photos (suggested sharing, printing promotions, photo book drafts, suggested photo books).
- Group similar faces – Turn on and off face grouping; if you don't want a robot scanning your photos to figure out the person that's in the shot, you can disable it here.
- Assistant cards – Picks the cards that show up in the Assistant menu of the Photos app (Creations, Rediscover this day, Recent highlights, Suggested Rotations, Suggested Archive).
- Memories – Memories are usually fun; seeing Google show you a photo of your kid as a baby can put a smile on your face as you start your day. But sometimes memories can suck—you go through a messy divorce or a loved one dies, and Google is there to remind you of their face. You can take those people out of your memories here. It doesn't delete

them from your account; you just won't see them show up in your feed.

Sharing Settings

- Shared libraries – Lets you see who can view your photos.
- Remove video from motion photos – Motion photos are nice—they're also big. If you prefer to just show the photo and not the video clip that goes with it, you can turn it off here.
- Remove geo location – Your photos have geo tags on them (unless you turn them off); that means when you share a photo, it might have things like your home address. If you don't want people to see that, then you can disable geo location with the people you are sharing it with.

Google apps

- Google Location settings – Lets you pick what apps can see your photos.
- Google Lens – Not a setting as much as instructions about how to use the app.

[7]

GOING BEYOND

This chapter will cover:

- System settings

If you want to take total control of your Pixel, then you need to know where the system settings are and what can and can't be changed there.

First the easy part: the system settings are located with the rest of your apps. Swipe up, and scroll down to "Settings."

There's a lot of settings here. Below are the available ones:

- Network & Internet
- Connected devices
- Apps
- Notification
- Battery
- Storage
- Sound & Vibration
- Display
- Wallpaper & Style
- Accessibility
- Privacy
- Location
- Safety & emergency
- Security
- Passwords & Accounts
- Digital Wellbeing & parental control
- Google
- System
- About phone
- Tips & support

I'll cover what each setting does in this chapter.

NETWORK & INTERNET

This setting, like most settings, does exactly what it sounds like: connects to the Internet. If you need to connect to a new wireless connection (or disconnect from one) you can do it here. Tapping on the current wireless lets you see other networks, and the toggle lets you switch it on and off.

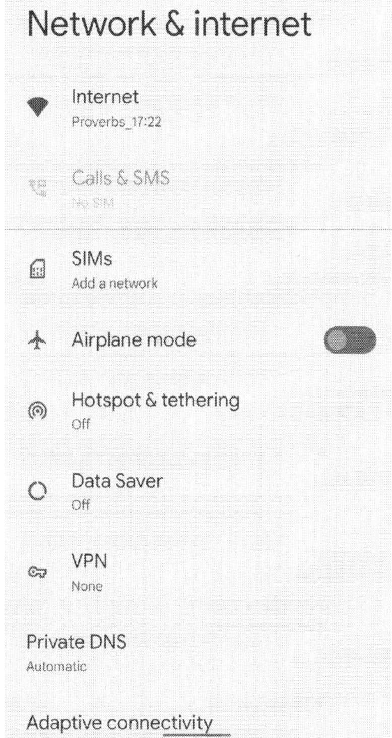

Mobile network is for your carrier (Verizon, AT&T, Sprint, etc.).

Data usage tells you how much data you've used; tapping on it gives you a deeper overview, so you can see exactly which apps used the data. Why is this important? For most, it probably won't be. I'll give an example of when it helped me: I work on the go a lot; I use the wireless on my phone to connect my laptop (which is called tethering); my MacBook was set to back-up to the cloud, and little did

I know it was doing this while connecting to my phone...20GB later, I was able to pinpoint what happened by looking at the data.

Below this is Hotspot & tethering. This is when you use your phone's data to connect other devices; you can use your phone's data plan, for example, to use the Internet on your iPad. Some carriers charge extra for this—mine (AT&T) includes it in the plan. To use it, tap the setting and turn it on, then name your network and password. From your other device, you find the network you set up, and connect.

Airplane mode is next. This setting turns off all wireless activity with a switch. So if your flying and they tell you to turn everything wireless of, you can do it with a switch.

Finally, Advanced is for doing some wireless connecting on a private network. This is not something a beginning user would need to do, and I'm not going to cover it, as the point of this book is to keep it ridiculously simple.

CONNECTED DEVICES

"Connected devices" is Google's way of saying Bluetooth. If you have something that connects via Bluetooth (such as a car radio or headphones) then tap "Pair new device." If you've previously paired something, then it will show below and you can simply tap it to reconnect.

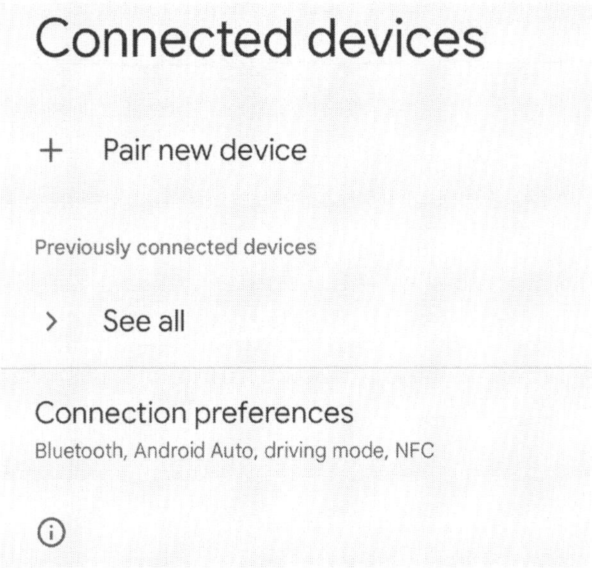

Connected devices

+ Pair new device

Previously connected devices

> See all

Connection preferences
Bluetooth, Android Auto, driving mode, NFC

APPS

Every app you download has different settings and permissions. A map app, for example, needs your permission to know your location. You can turn these permissions on and off here. Does it really matter? App makers can't abuse it, right? Sort of. Here's an example: a few months ago, a popular ride-sharing app made headlines because it wanted to know where passengers were after they left the ride, so they could promote different restaurants and stores and make even more money. Many felt this was both greedy and an invasion of privacy; if you are of the latter stance, then you could go in here and stop sharing your location.

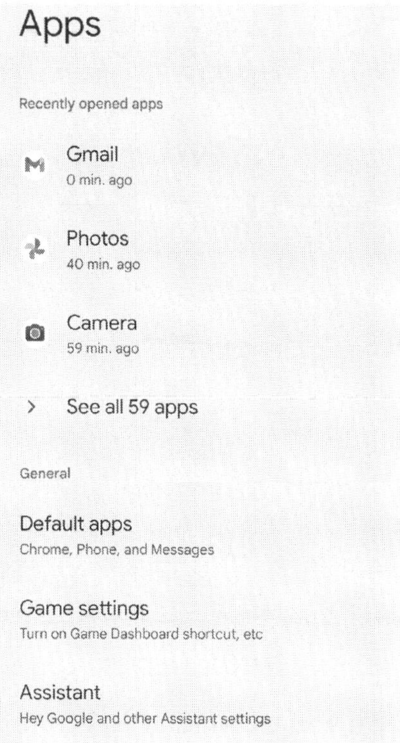

You can also use this setting to turn on Game Shortcuts.

NOTIFICATIONS

Want to see the notifications you accidently dismissed? You can find that in the Notifications settings. You can also decide the priority people get when you get notifications. Bubbles let's conversations come in like floating icons; you can turn that on and off here.

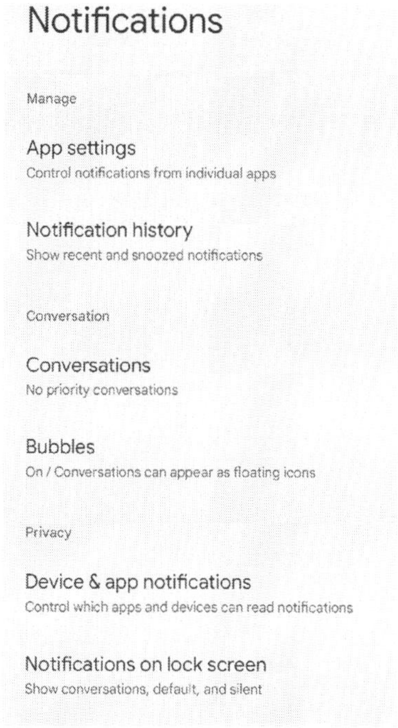

Notifications

Manage

App settings
Control notifications from individual apps

Notification history
Show recent and snoozed notifications

Conversation

Conversations
No priority conversations

Bubbles
On / Conversations can appear as floating icons

Privacy

Device & app notifications
Control which apps and devices can read notifications

Notifications on lock screen
Show conversations, default, and silent

BATTERY

The battery setting is more about analytics than settings you can change. There are some settings here you can edit—you can put your phone in battery saving mode, for example. This setting is more useful if your battery is draining too quickly; it helps you troubleshoot what's going on so you can get more life from your phone.

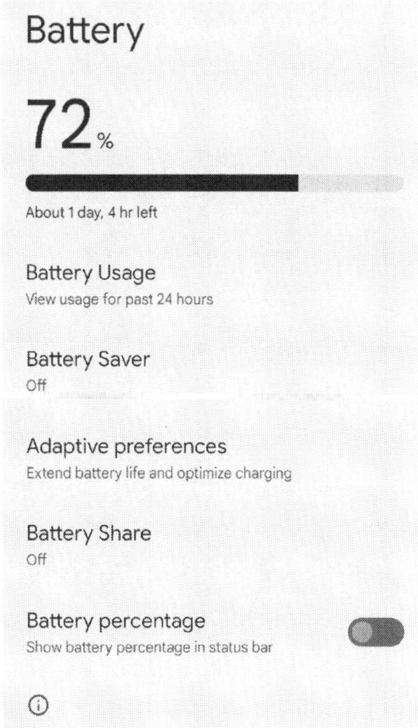

A Smarter Battery

Google's AI can extend into your battery life. By default, the Pixel automatically will go into Battery Saver mode when you get to 10% battery remaining. That's great. But you can also set it to go on based on your routine. So Google's AI predicts your daily habits and adjust the battery accordingly.

To use this mode, go to the System Settings app, then tap Battery and Battery Saver. Next tap Set a Schedule. Tap the option that says "Based on your routine."

STORAGE

The Pixel has no expandable storage for SD; that means whatever you buy for your phone, that's the amount you have. You can't upgrade it later.

When you first get your phone, storage won't be a big issue, but once you start taking photos (which are larger than you think) and installing apps, it's going to go very quickly.

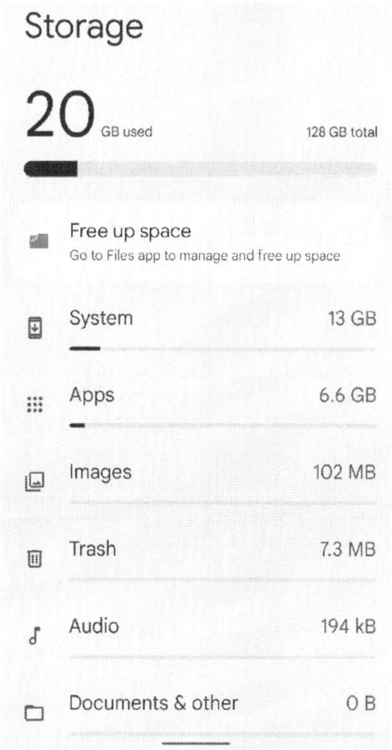

Storage
20 GB used
128 GB total
Free up space
Go to Files app to manage and free up space
System 13 GB
Apps 6.6 GB
Images 102 MB
Trash 7.3 MB
Audio 194 kB
Documents & other 0 B

The storage setting helps you manage this. It shows you what's taking up storage, so you can decide if you want to delete things. Just tap on any of the subsections and follow the instructions for what to do to save space.

SOUND & VIBRATION

There's a volume button on the side of your phone, so why would you need to open up a setting for it?! This setting lets you get more specific about your volume.

For example, you may want your alarm to ring super loud in the morning, but you want your music to play very low.

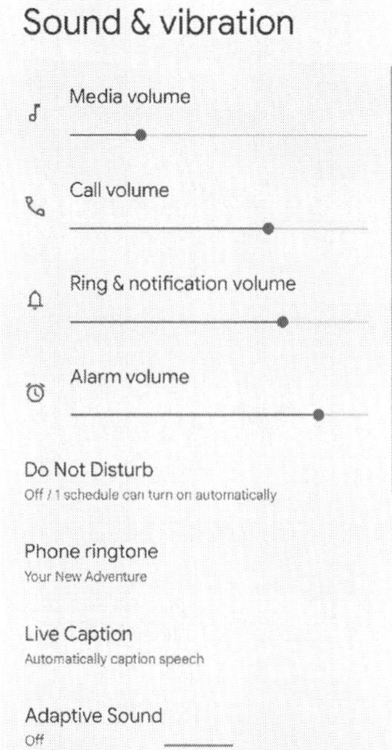

DISPLAY

As with most of the settings, almost all the main features of the Display setting can be changed outside of the app. If you tap "Advanced," however, you'll see some settings not in other places. These include changing colors and font sizes.

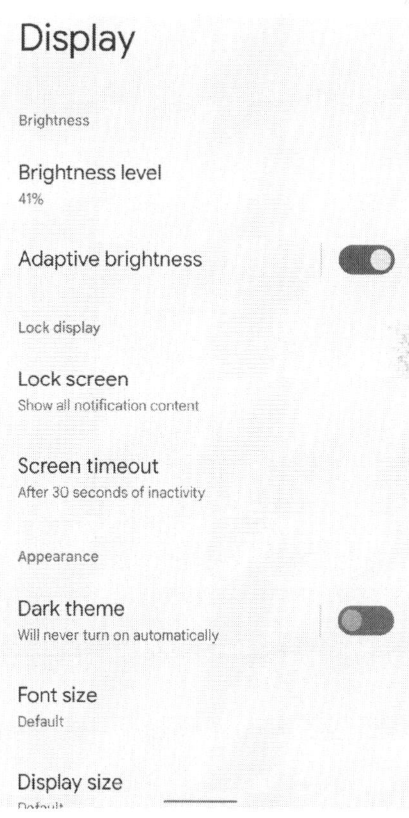

WALLPAPER & STYLE

This setting is nothing more than the setting that comes when you access wallpaper from your homescreen.

ACCESSIBILITY

Do you hate phones because the text is too small, the colors are all wrong, you can't hear anything? Or something else? That's where accessibility can help. This is where you make changes to the device to make it easier on your eyes or ears.

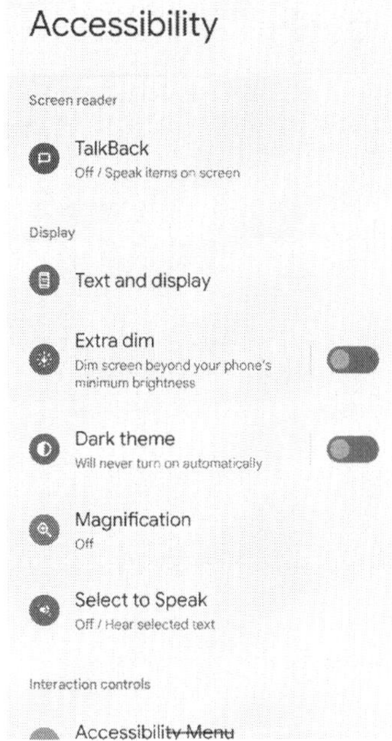

PRIVACY

Like Location Control (covered below), Privacy settings got a big upgrade in Android 12. It's so big, it now fills an entire section in the settings.

Go to System > Privacy and tap "Advanced" to see all of them.

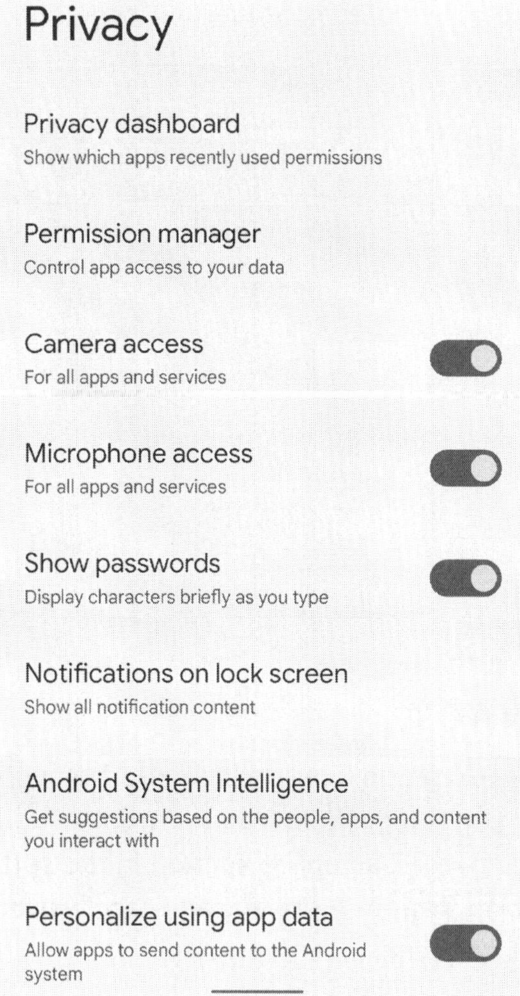

The biggest upgrade is the ability to customize what apps see what; it's no longer all or nothing. You can refine exactly how much or how little each app can see.

The Privacy Dashboard is one of the easiest ways to see what apps are doing. In the example below, it shows in the past 24 hours, most my apps were using my location.

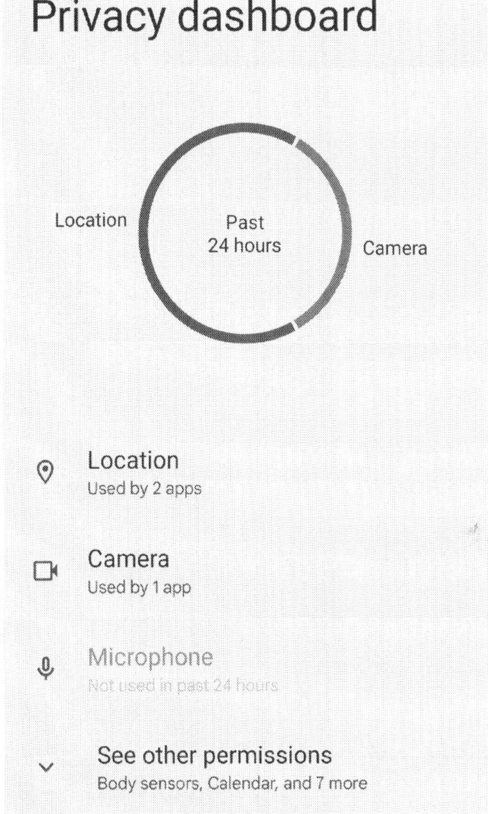

Tapping on Location will reveal what apps were using the location.

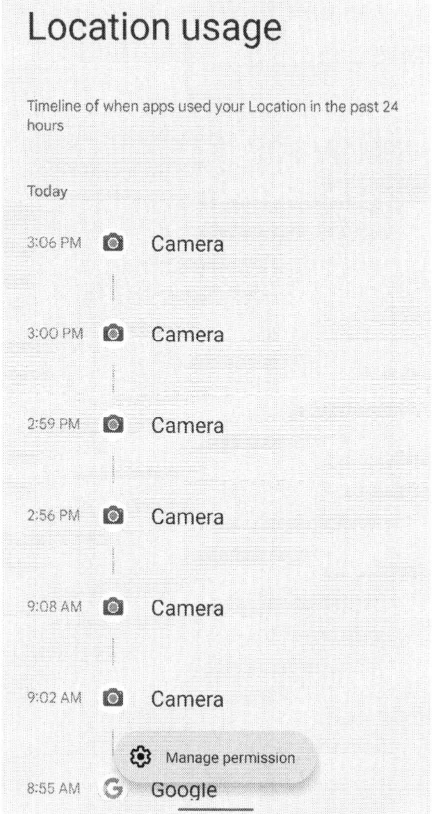

You can then tap on Manage permissions (either on this screen or the main settings screen) to disable location sharing.

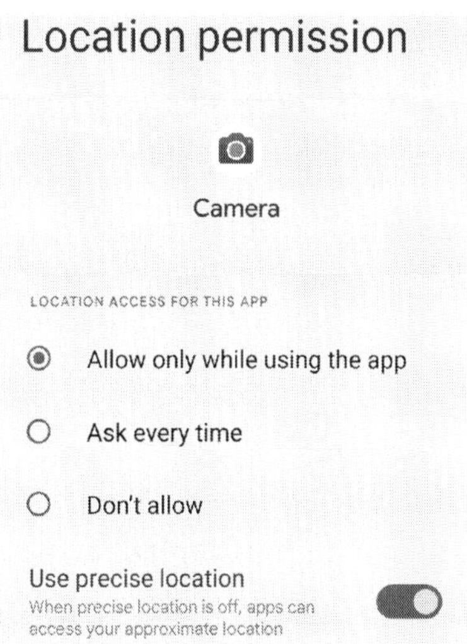

SECURITY

If you want to change your lock screen, add an additional fingerprint, or turn on / off the find your phone setting, you can do it here.

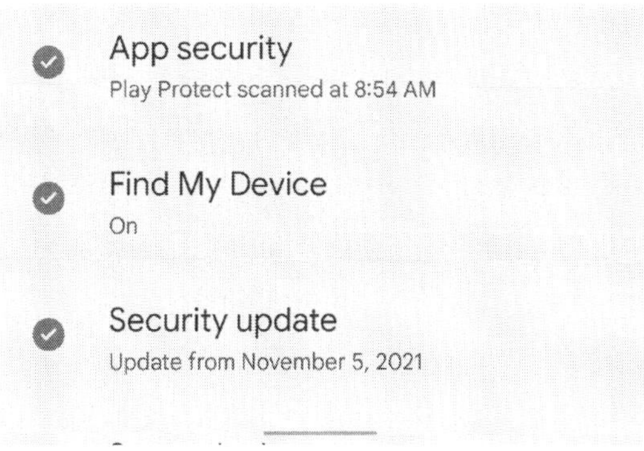

LOCATION

In the past, Location Control was an all or nothing feature—you'd decide if an app could see you all the time or none of the time. That's nice for privacy, but not nice for when you actually need someone to know your location—like when you are getting picked up by a ride app like Lyft. The new Android OS adds a new option for while you are using the app. So, for example, a ride app can only see your location while you are using the app; once the ride is over, they can no longer see what you are doing.

To pick what location an app can see, go to System > Location and select the app, then tap when they can see your location.

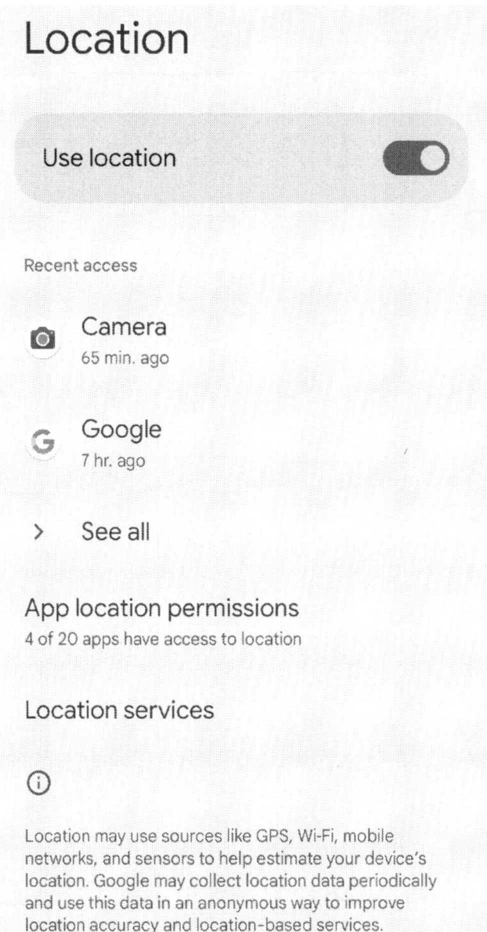
Location
Use location
Recent access
Camera
65 min. ago
Google
7 hr. ago
See all
App location permissions
4 of 20 apps have access to location
Location services
Location may use sources like GPS, Wi-Fi, mobile networks, and sensors to help estimate your device's location. Google may collect location data periodically and use this data in an anonymous way to improve location accuracy and location-based services.

SAFETY & EMERGENCY

These settings let you add important details about you—like your blood type; they also let you enable safety features—like crash detection if your mobile device detects a motion that is common with car accidents.

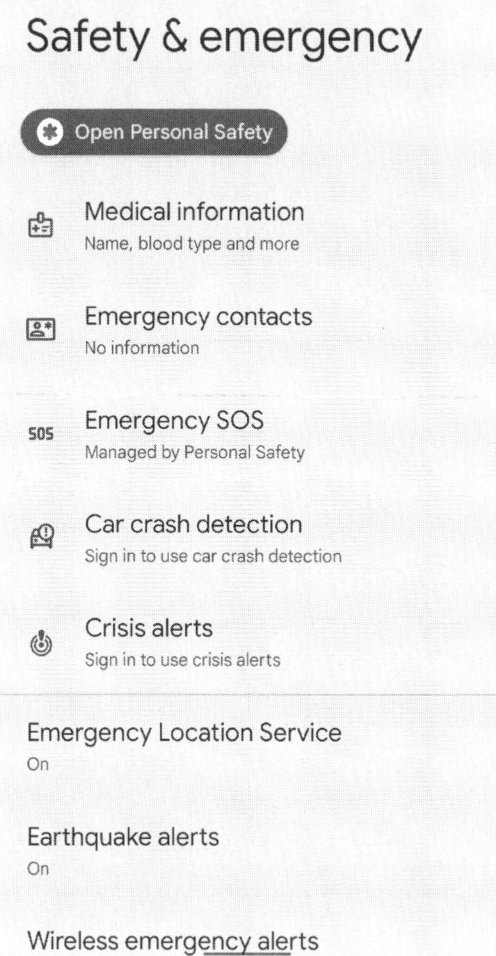

Car Crash Detection

Nobody hopes to use this feature, but you'll be thankful for it if the unthinkable happens. With crash detection turned on, your phone will alert emergency services if it detects you have been in a car accident. It won't call immediately, it will give you a prompt to tell you what it's doing, so if it's a mistake, you can stop it. To turn it on, go to Settings > Safety & emergency > Car crash detection.

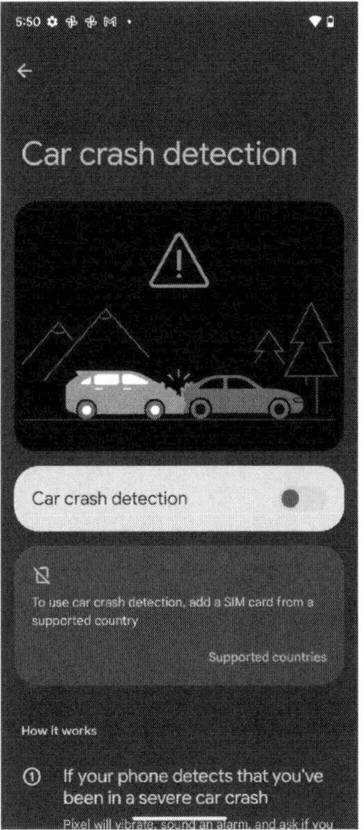

ACCESSIBILITY

Do you hate phones because the text is too small, the colors are all wrong, you can't hear anything? Or something else? That's where accessibility can help. This is where you make changes to the device to make it easier on your eyes or ears.

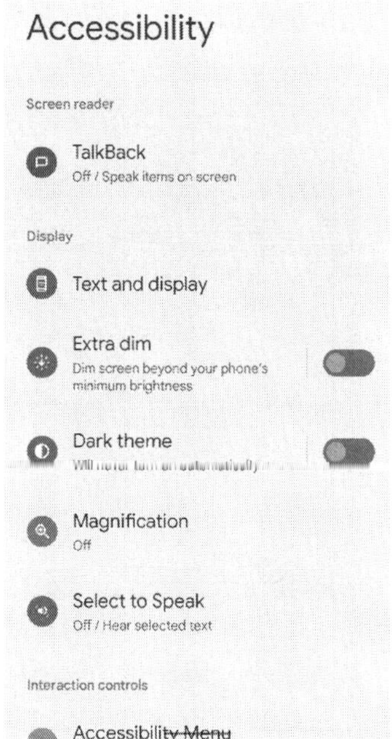

DIGITAL WELLBEING

Digital Wellbeing is my least favorite feature on the Pixel phone; now when my wife says "You spend too much time on your phone"—she can actually prove it!

The purpose of the setting is to help you manage your time more. It lets you know your spending 12 hours a day updating your social media with memes of cats, and "hopefully" make you feel like perhaps you shouldn't do that.

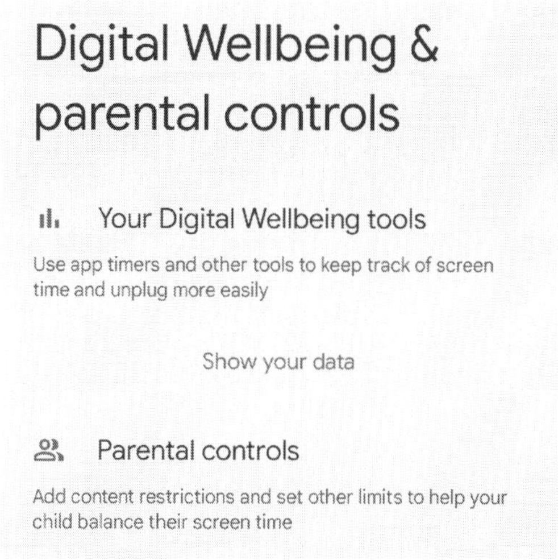

Digital Wellbeing & parental controls

Your Digital Wellbeing tools

Use app timers and other tools to keep track of screen time and unplug more easily

Show your data

Parental controls

Add content restrictions and set other limits to help your child balance their screen time

GOOGLE

Google is where you will go to manage any Google device connected with your phone. If you are using a Google watch, for example; or a Chromecast.

SYSTEM

System is important for one very important reason: system updates. If you don't have your phone set to download updates automatically, then you'll have to do it manually here.

Tap the "Advanced" button.

This gives you a menu with more features. One is the "System update." If there's an update available, it will say it. If it says it, then tap it.

You'll have to restart your phone before it downloads.

Security update available

This update fixes critical bugs and improves the performance and stability of your Pixel 3. If you download updates over the cellular network or while roaming, additional charges may apply.

Update size: 108.5 MB

You can also change the language in this setting as well as make changes to gestures and put limits on users.

ABOUT PHONE

This is where you will find general information about your phone. Such as the OS you are running, the kind of phone you have, IP address, etc. It's more of an FYI, but there are a few settings here that you can change.

TIPS & SUPPORT

This isn't really a setting. It's just tips and support. You can also talk with support here.

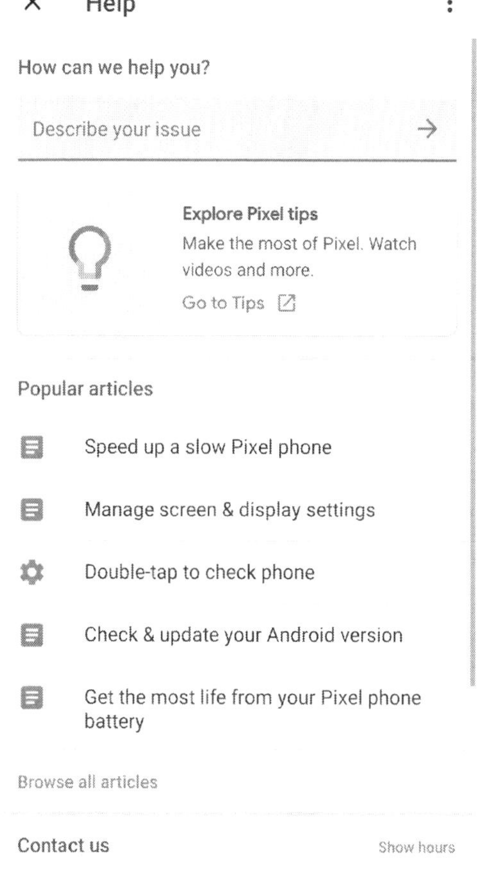

BONUS BOOK: USING GMAIL

INTRODUCTION

Email as a communication tool has been used since the 1960s. Commercial use of email is still relatively young.

In the early years, email was usually tied to a paid service like AOL. It wasn't long before companies like Hotmail came along and offered the service for free. Dozens of email providers have come and gone—I bet you've even used a few of them (anyone remember Juno mail out there? For a college kid with no money, Juno was the best thing since Top Ramen!)

Today, email is dominated by one company: Google. Estimates show that over 50% of all people with email use Gmail! If you picked up this book, you probably have one or are considering getting one.

For its email service, Gmail is easy enough to use—compose email, send email, done! But there's more to Gmail than sending and receiving email.

How do you get not-Spam emails to stop showing up as Spam, for example? What on Earth are labels? And how do you get email forwarded to another inbox?

If you want to be a power user, then read on!

[1] GMAIL CRASH COURSE

This chapter will cover:

- Overview of features
- Where things are

I'm going to go quickly through this chapter. Don't worry! This is just a high-level overview. I'll slow down in future chapters to drill a little deeper into different subjects.

One thing to note: this book only covers the desktop version of Gmail; the mobile version is very much the same, but there are a few extra things—notably swipe gestures. Once you understand the desktop version, you should have no problem with the mobile app.

First things first: How do you get an email? If you already have one, great! Skip this part! In fact, you might find yourself skipping around a lot. This book is for beginning and more experienced users alike, so if you've already been using Gmail for a while, then you may jump ahead.

As a side note, you can have as many email addresses as you like—personally, I have a family one, a business one, and a bogus one (which I use to fill out forms for companies I'm not sure if I trust). So if you already have one, feel free to create another!

To get started, go to gmail.com. You'll be greeted by a very simple webpage. It's asking you to sign in. How do you sign in when you don't have an account? You don't, obviously! Just click the Create account button under the sign-in box to get started. (Note: Anytime you need to access email after you have created an email, start at this page):

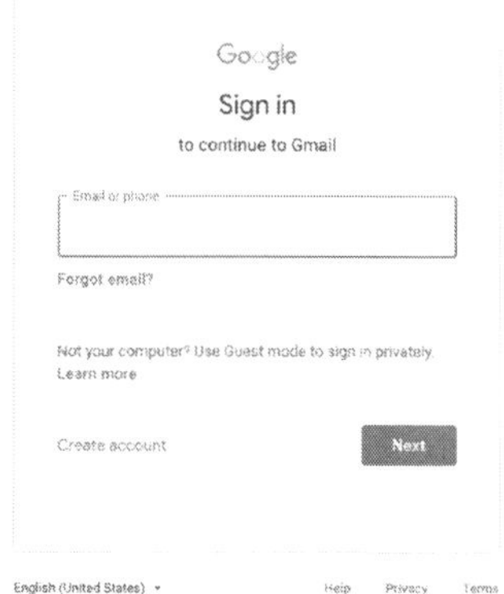

When you select Create account, it's going to ask if it's for yourself or a business:

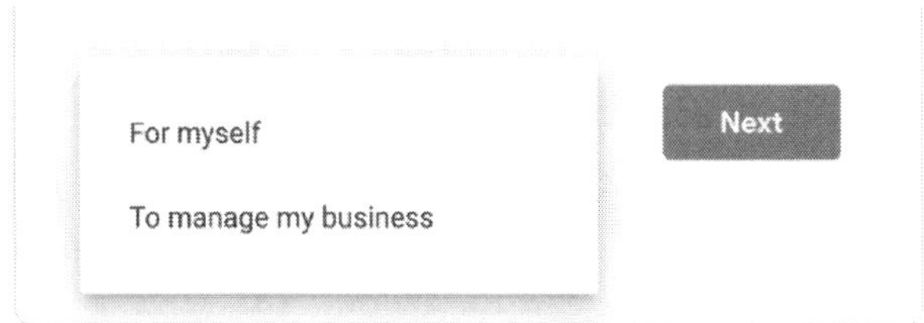

If you select business, Google's going to sell you on having a business account. That lets you use Gmail, but have your company's @ extension. Many businesses use the free personal version for their business—especially when they're just getting started.

Next, fill out the Google Account info, and hit Next:

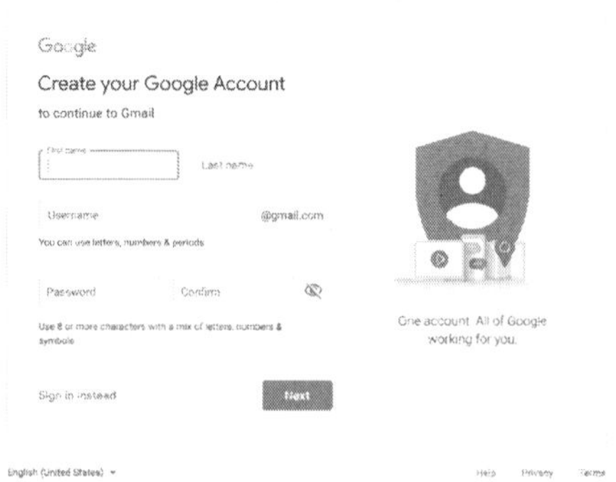

Remember I said an account could be bogus? Here I am creating one for Jonah Simms (in case you don't know, that's the name of a fictional character on the NBC show Superstore):

Turns out I'm not the only person who is a fan of Jonah Simms—my guess is there actually is a Jonah Simms in the world. In any case, my first choice for email is gone:

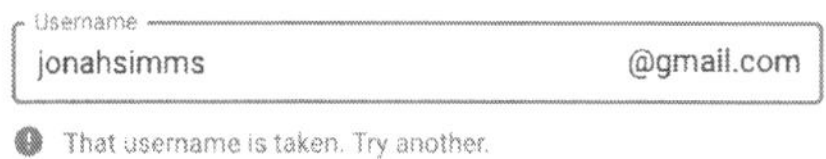

You might get the same error message—with over a billion Gmail accounts out there, many usernames are taken. Just keep thinking of new ones until you find one that's not taken. I just added a number 2 to mine.

Next, Gmail will ask some more personal information about you:

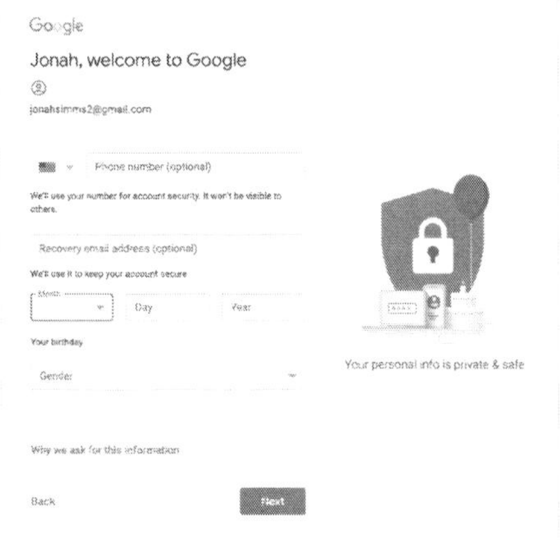

Why do they want to know this? If you really want to know, click the hyperlink, and it will tell you:

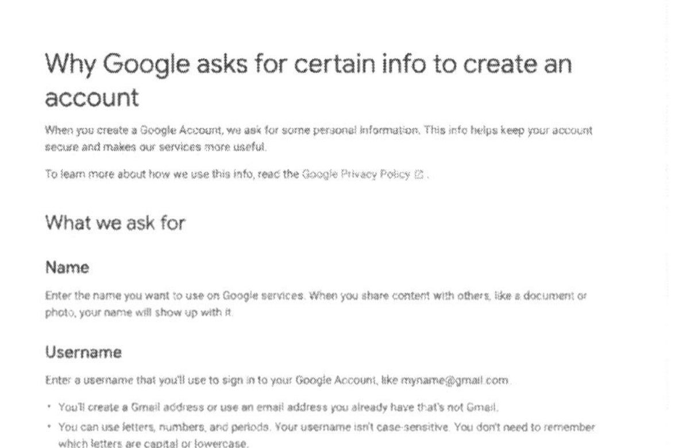

Why Google asks for certain info to create an account

When you create a Google Account, we ask for some personal information. This info helps keep your account secure and makes our services more useful.

To learn more about how we use this info, read the Google Privacy Policy.

What we ask for

Name

Enter the name you want to use on Google services. When you share content with others, like a document or photo, your name will show up with it.

Username

Enter a username that you'll use to sign in to your Google Account, like myname@gmail.com.

- You'll create a Gmail address or use an email address you already have that's not Gmail.
- You can use letters, numbers, and periods. Your username isn't case-sensitive. You don't need to remember which letters are capital or lowercase.

Most the fields are optional. Even the gender field has an option for not saying—and one for creating a custom gender:

Privacy is big with Google. The next page has a very lengthy Terms of Service. Is creating a bogus account in violation of these terms? Feel free to read this lengthy legal document to find out!

Or be like everyone else and scroll until the end and hit I agree:

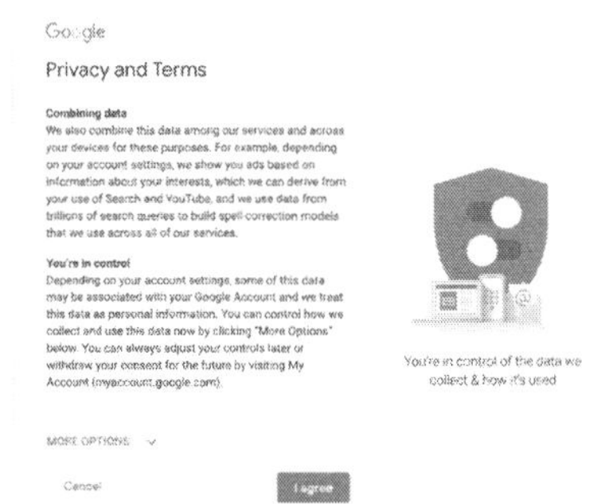

Congrats! You now have email!

When you hit Next, Gmail will ask what kind of view you want. There are three. The first is the default view that most people select:

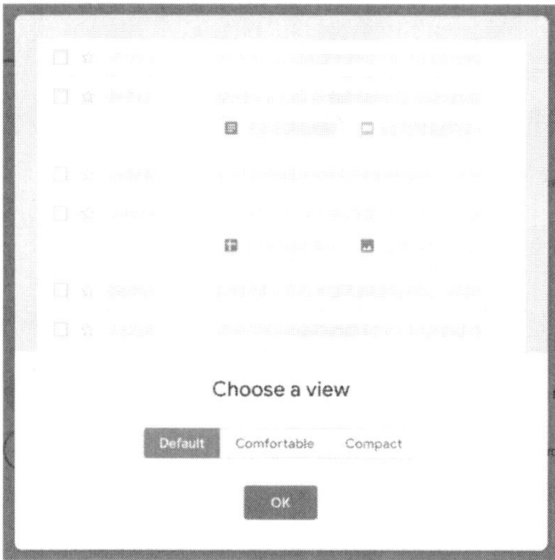

It's simple and it shows attachments—by that, I mean you can open attachments without opening the email.

Next is Comfortable; it's a little simpler. That open attachment option is gone and you'll see instead a paperclip next to emails with attachments:

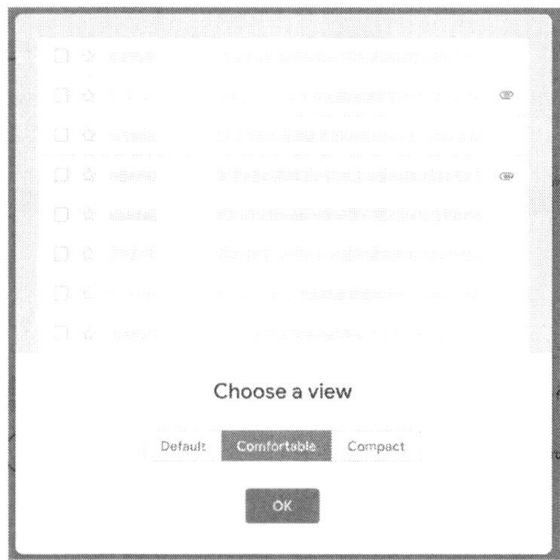

The last option is Compact. This is very similar to the Comfortable theme, but it's more compressed so you can see more emails on your screen. None work better than the other—it's just a preference (one that can be changed). When you have picked the one you want, select OK:

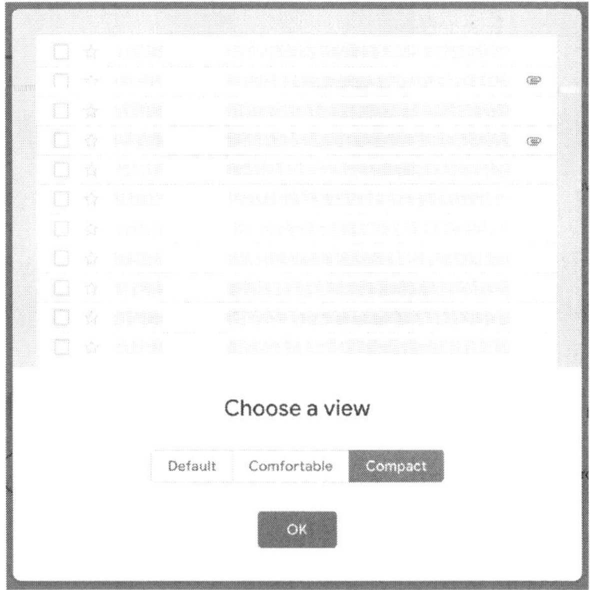

You'll now have access to all of your email—it's going to be empty right now, obviously:

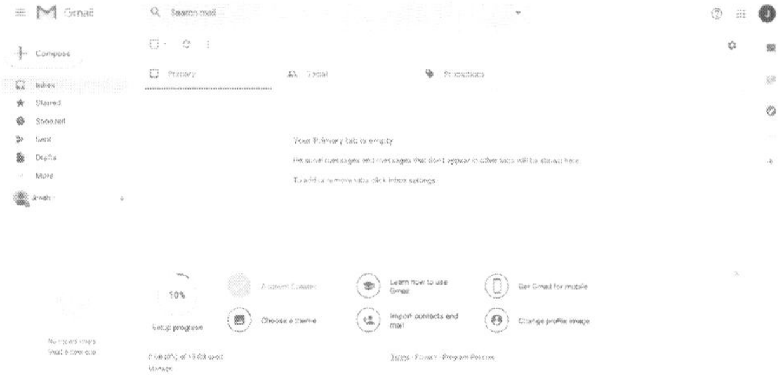

The menu on the left side is the one you'll use the most. Very quickly (again, we'll cover this more later), you'll see your main Inbox, Starred mail (this means you've basically flagged email to go in a special area), Snoozed (email that will return to your email at a later date), Sent, Drafts (if you accidently close an email before its sent, it will go here), and finally, More:

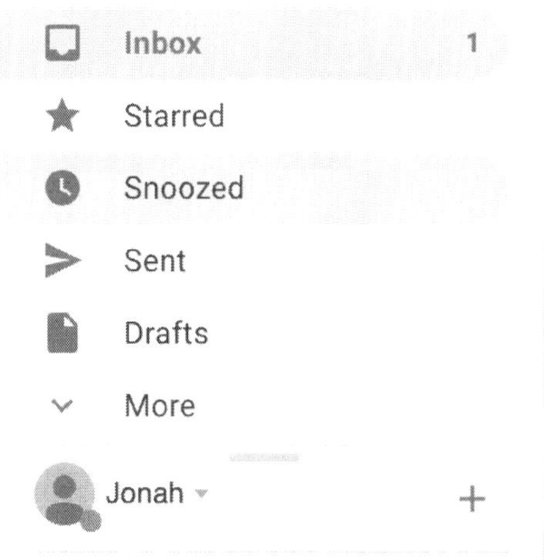

Selecting More brings up a larger menu. The thing you'll use the most here is probably Spam and Trash (where deleted emails go). Why would you use Spam? It's not uncommon for important emails to go here. It's a good idea to check it every day or every other day. If you aren't entering contests 24/7, then you shouldn't get a lot of Spam:

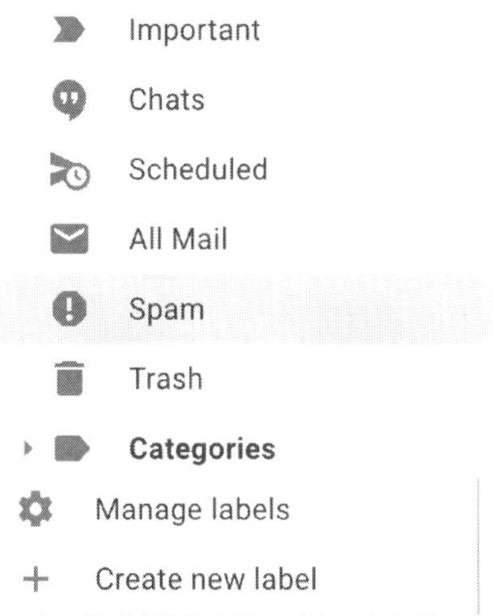

Above this menu is the Compose button; you'll click that to start a new email:

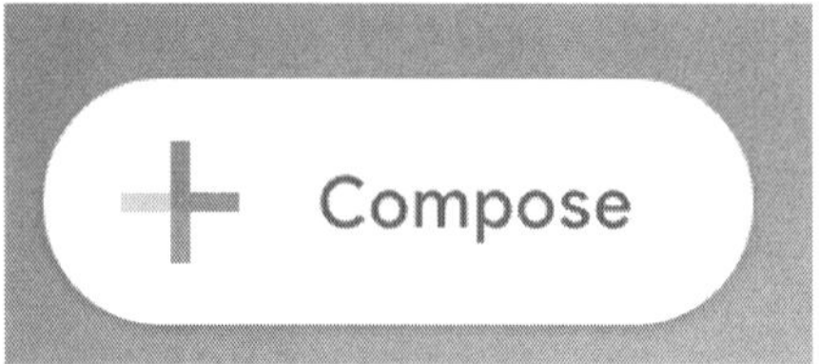

Next to Compose is a button with three lines. That expands and collapses your menu. Click it once and watch it collapse and become more narrow. Click it again and it goes back to normal:

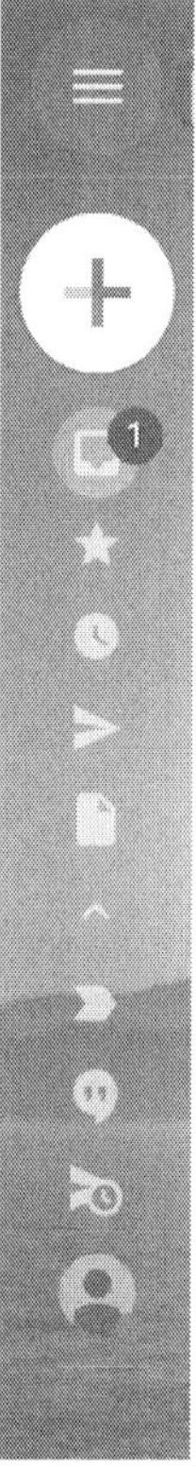

Below the menu is a dialog box with a quotation. That's where you go to start a Hangout (a Hangout is like a video call—another free service from Google), or chat with someone:

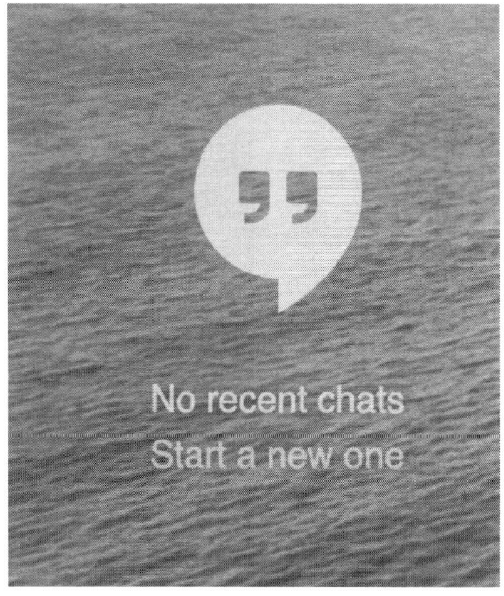

To the right of Hangouts, you can see how much space you've used. Unless you send a lot of attachments, you'll probably never exceed it. If you do, you can buy more space very cheaply. As of this writing, you can get 100 GB for 20 bucks a year.

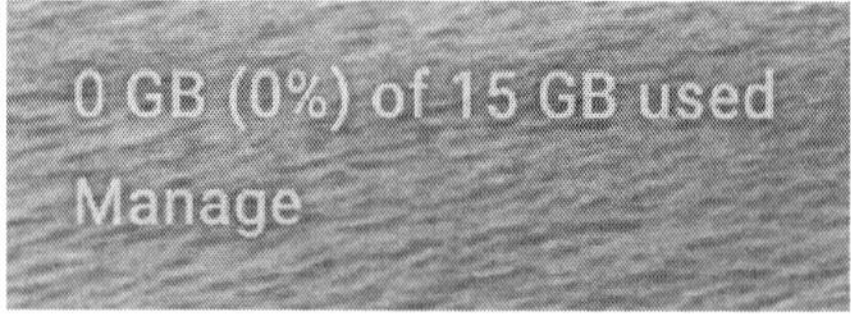

To the far, lower right, you can see your account activity. This tells you all the sessions that are signed in. Let's say you went to a public library and forgot to sign out. Yikes, right?! Go here and just click Details:

If there's a remote session in place—meaning someone is using your account from a distant place, then there's going to be an option to sign out. And speaking of signing out—how do you do that?! Go to the upper right corner. If you have a profile picture, then it will show your beautiful face. If not, it will have your abbreviation. When you click on that, you can Sign out:

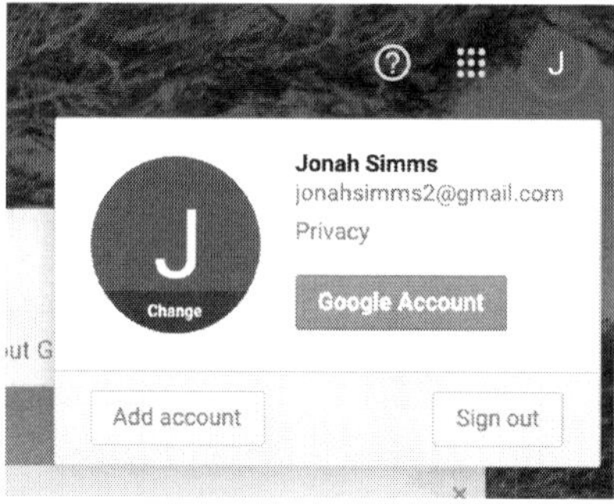

Next to that is a button with nine dots. Click that and you'll see some of Google's most popular apps. Since you have gmail, you have access to all of them:

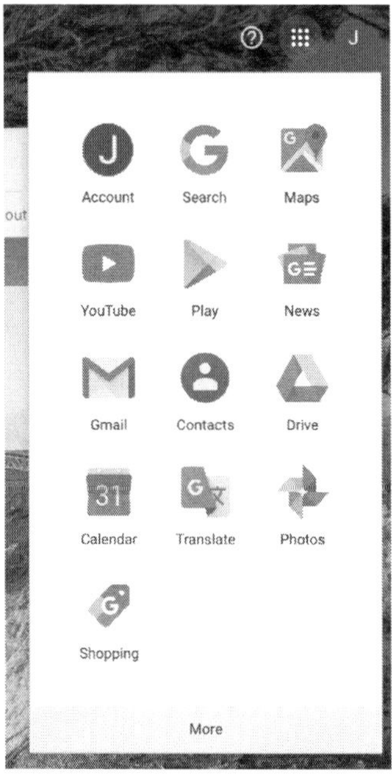

Just below that, you'll see a configure button. This is where you can do things like change the theme we set up earlier. We are going to spend a lot of time in this area. For now, just know where it is:

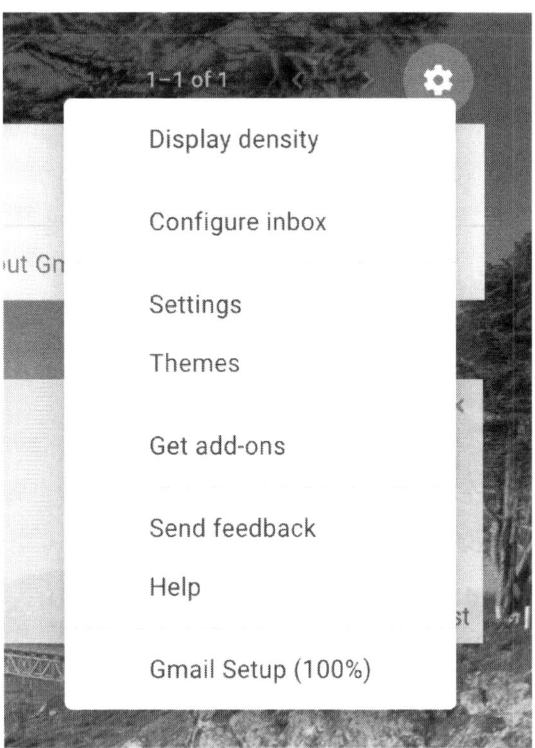

On the right side is the side menu. Here, you can get to your calendar, your idea book, your tasks, or you can add Gmail plugin apps (i.e. third party apps that tie into Gmail):

Finally, at the top is the search menu. This is where you can search your mail:

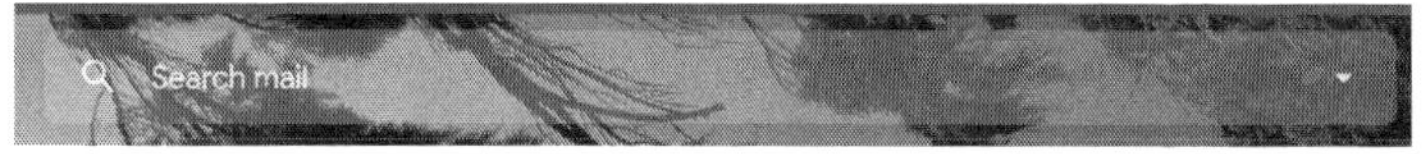

Near the bottom of your inbox, you'll see a 10% setup progress. What does that mean? You have email! Aren't you all setup?! Technically, yes. This is Google's way of helping you learn the email ropes. It actually is helpful, and you can do it very quickly.

The first option is theme:

Theme puts an image on your inbox to make it a little more personal. Go ahead and pick one! Even if you haven't hit save yet, you'll see a preview:

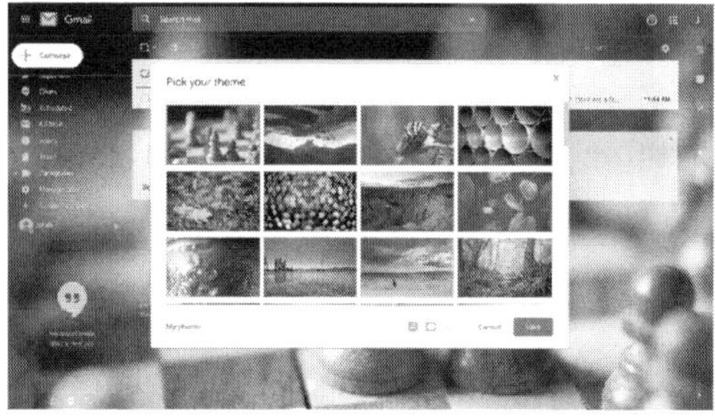

There are a few options on the bottom to help make the image easier to see behind your email. The first (the A button) makes the email area either dark or light. (You can change all of this later!)

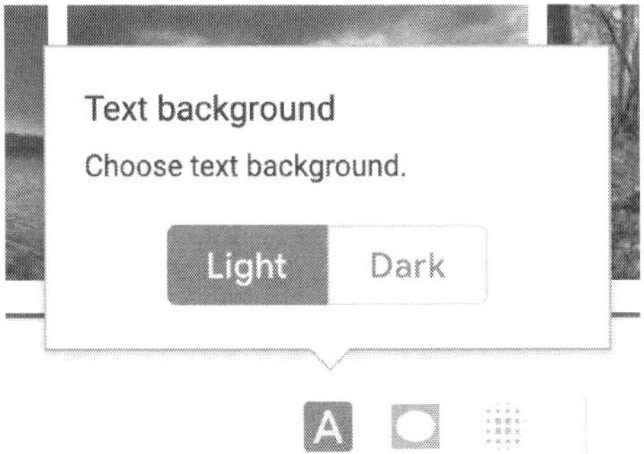

When you toggle it, you'll notice the background of your email is changing:

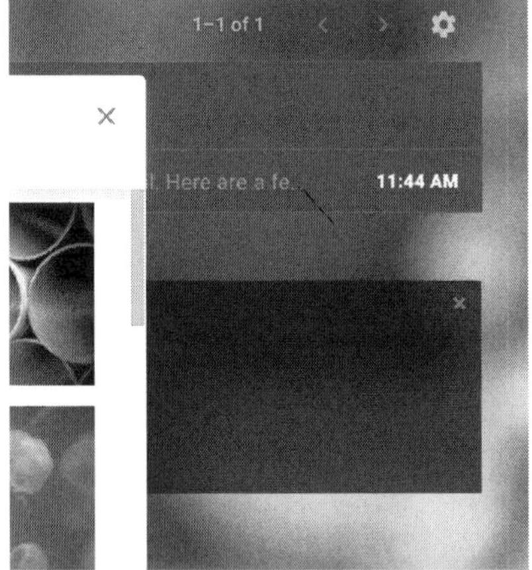

Next is vignette, which just makes the corners of the image darker. Sliding it to the right will adjust the darkness:

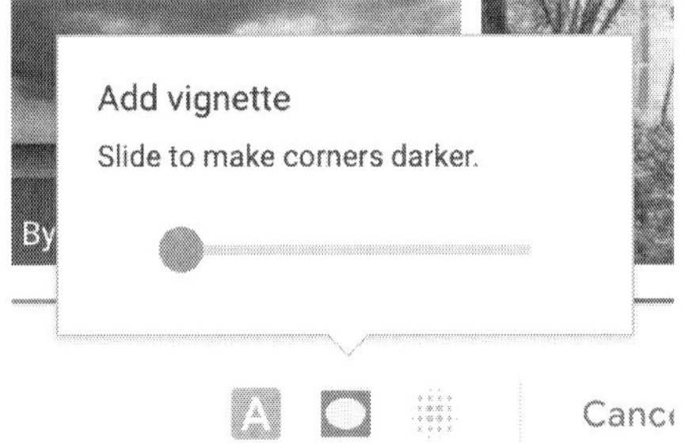

Finally, you can apply a blur. Personally, I like this feature best; when you have a really sharp image, it can make it harder to see text on the screen. Blurring the image makes emails and text stand out more, in my opinion.

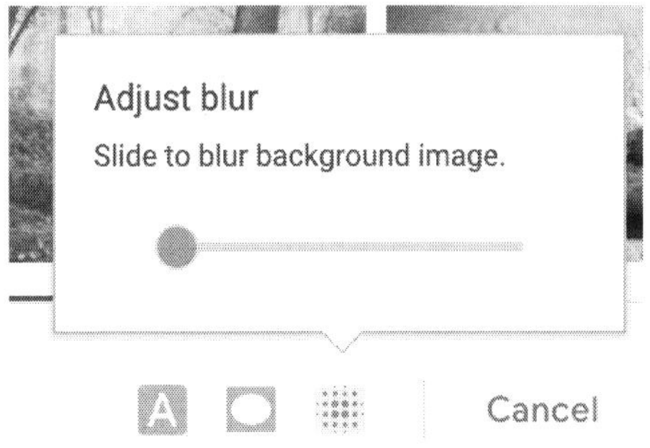

Once you hit save, you'll notice that this event is not done. You are one step closer to completing Gmail's quick setup!

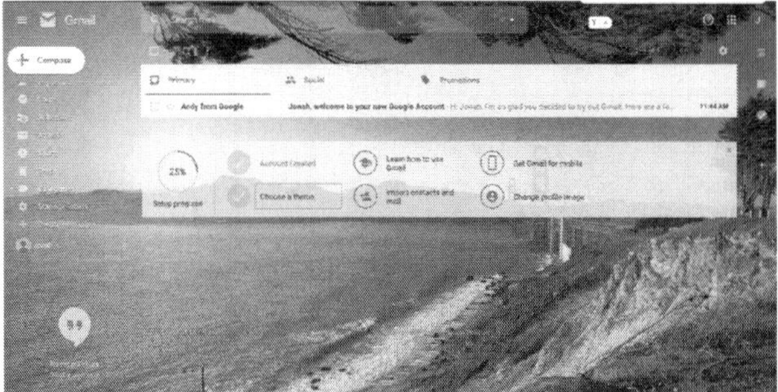

The next option is Learn how to use Gmail. Click on that and it brings up a help box. I do recommend spending a few seconds here. It has some good tips.

Close it and the activity is done!

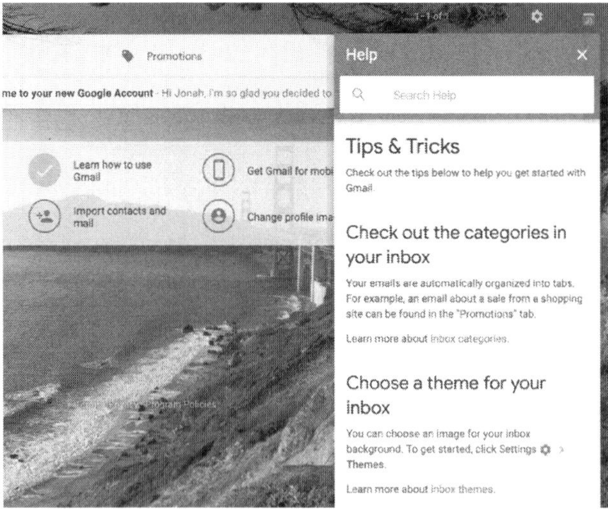

If you already have an email (such as a work email) and you want to import over all the contacts, click the Import contacts option; if you just want this to show that you've completed the setup, then click it and then cancel it:

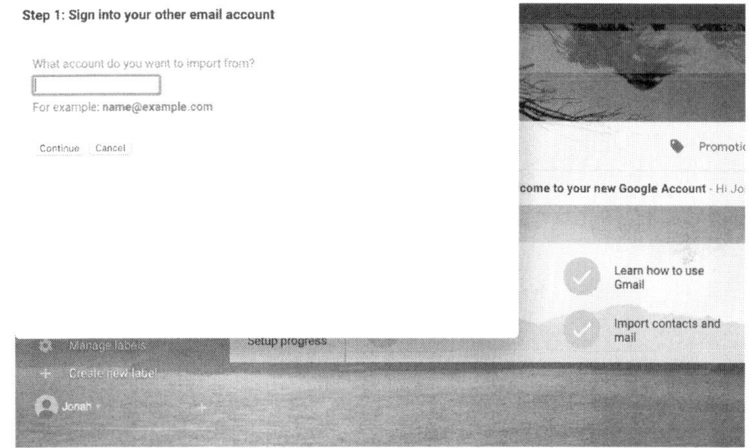

This is going to walk you through the quick and easy steps to connecting the email. In most cases, it's just a matter of signing into your email:

Getting the mobile app is next. The mobile app lets you read email on your phone or tablet—you can also get a mobile-friendly version of Gmail by going to Gmail.com from your browser. Using a native app, however, let's you get notifications of new mail in real time:

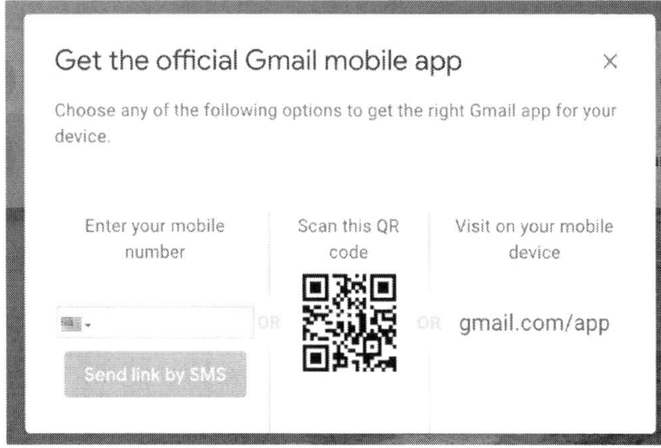

Next, select a profile photo. This is what people see when they get a message from you. You don't have to pick one, but I do recommend it. Sometimes people don't know who you are until they see your face:

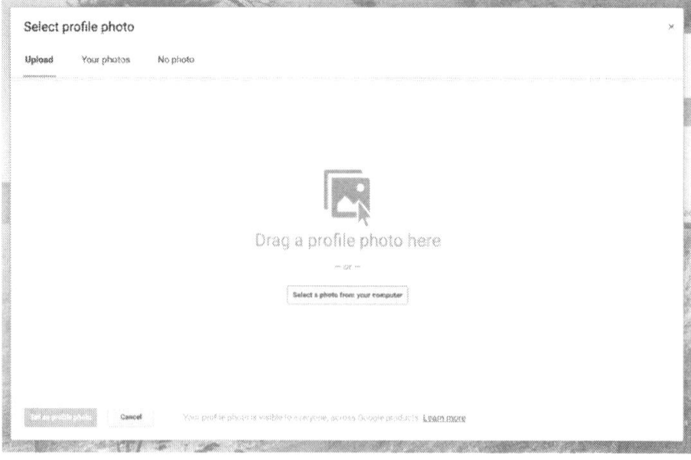

Once you complete that, you'll get the 100% badge of honor!

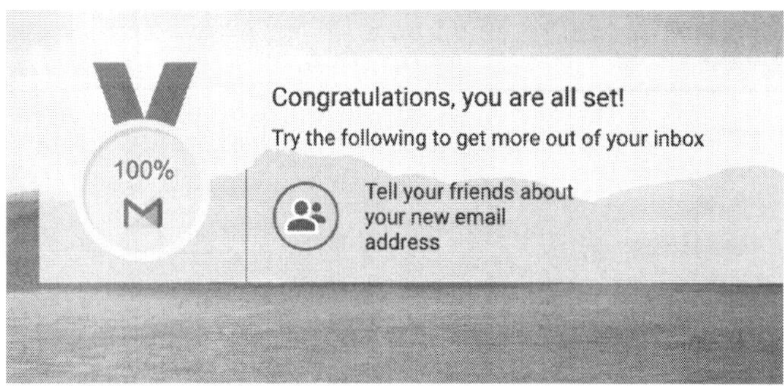
Congratulations, you are all set!
Try the following to get more out of your inbox
100%
Tell your friends about your new email address

[2]

How to Send and Receive Mail

This chapter will cover:

- Sending email
- Adding attachments
- Reading email
- Adding labels
- Adding contacts
- Searching for email

HOW TO SEND EMAIL

Now that you know your way around, let's have some fun and send an email.

Email comes naturally for most people. But there's more inside the email then just compose and send. There's a lot of extra formatting you can do.

In case this is your first time using Gmail, or your first time using email, click the Compose button on the upper left hand side:

This opens up the New Message window:

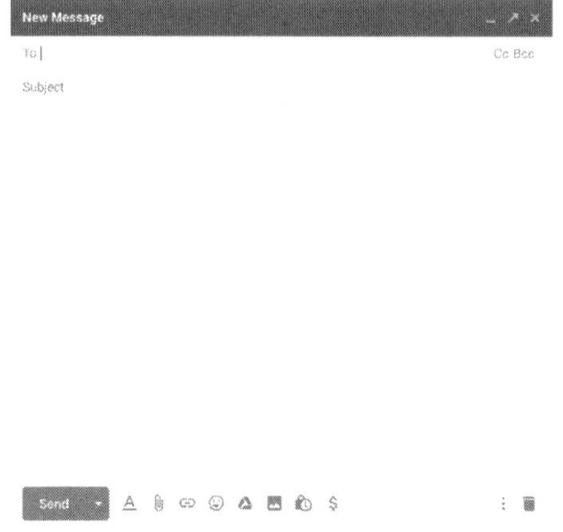

Click the arrow next to the X in the upper left corner. That makes the message larger; click it again to return to normal size:

By default, all you see is the "To" field. Enter someone's email here; if you want to send a CC or BCC, then click the button that says CC or BCC:

Cc Bcc

CC is a carbon copy—a copy of the email that will go to a person that you think needs to see the email, but does not necessarily need to reply. A BCC is a blind carbon copy. This means other people cannot see who you sent it to. If you are sending a huge list, one hack is to send it to yourself and BCC everyone else. This way everyone gets what you are sending, but they can't see everyone else on the list.

To

Cc |

Bcc

Subject

When you start typing in the body, you'll see the format bar. If you don't see it hit the A next to Send. You can add emojis to the subject, but you can't change the formatting here—for example, you can't Bold the subject.

The non-format menu is at the bottom of the message. I already said what "A" does. The paper-clip attaches a file, the one next to that inserts a link into the message (you can also highlight a word and do CTRL+K for this), the face inserts an emoji, the triangle is Google Drive (if you have a file you want to attach that's in Google Drive versus your computer), next to that is to insert a picture, and finally, the little button with the clock puts the email in confidential mode.

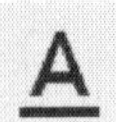      

Confidential mode is James Bond for email! This message will self-destruct kind of stuff! It takes away the ability for the person to forward, print, or copy the message. You can also set limits on when it expires, and require a code.

Confidential mode

Recipients won't have the option to forward, copy, print, or download this email. Learn more

SET EXPIRATION

Expires in 1 week ▾ Fri, Aug 16, 2019

REQUIRE PASSCODE

All passcodes will be generated by Google. ?

◉ No SMS passcode ○ SMS passcode

Cancel Save

Finally, the money key lets you either send money via email or ask for money. You just need to add a debit card. It's kind of like Google's version of PayPal, but without the fees:

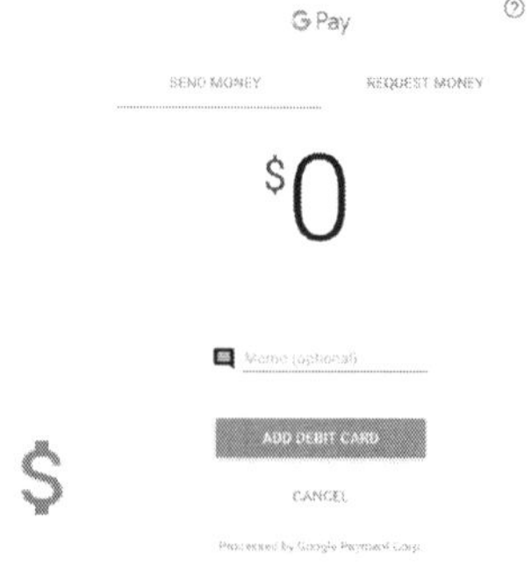

The three dots in the bottom left corner opens up the email menu; this lets you do things like spell

check and print. You can also add a label, which we'll cover more in the next section.

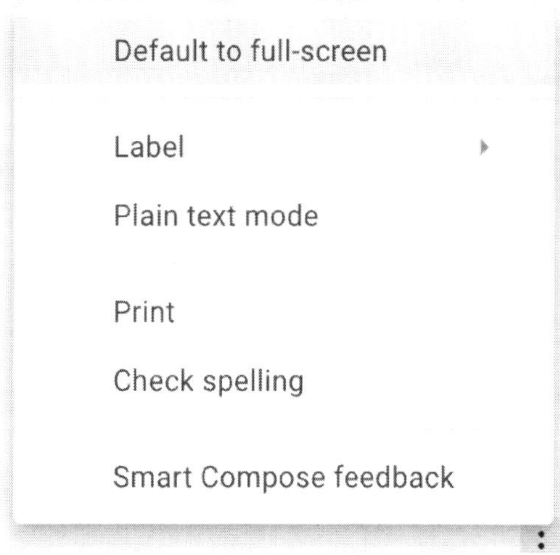

Finally, the trash icon deletes the message:

If you accidently close the message (or if you do it on purpose), go to that side menu and select Drafts. It will be there waiting for you. Just click it and the email will reopen.

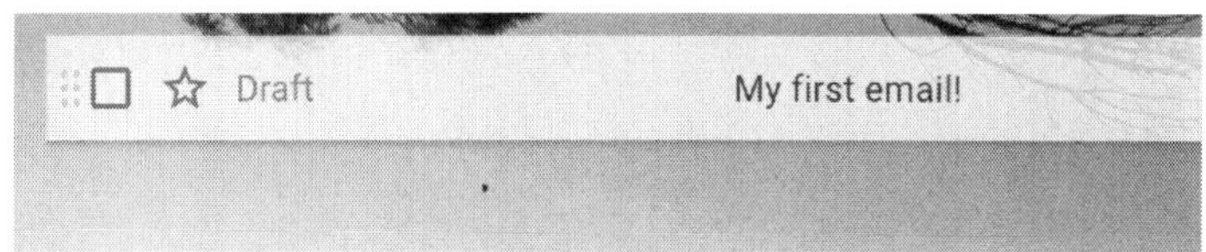

When you are ready to send the email, click the blue Send. If you want to schedule it (so it sends later), then just hit the arrow next to it:

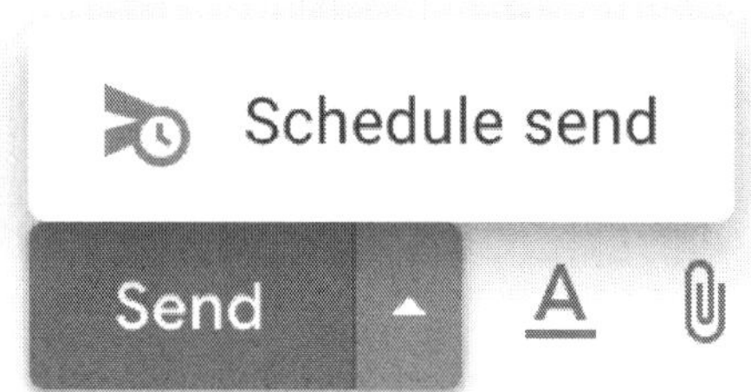

Google will show you common times to schedule it:

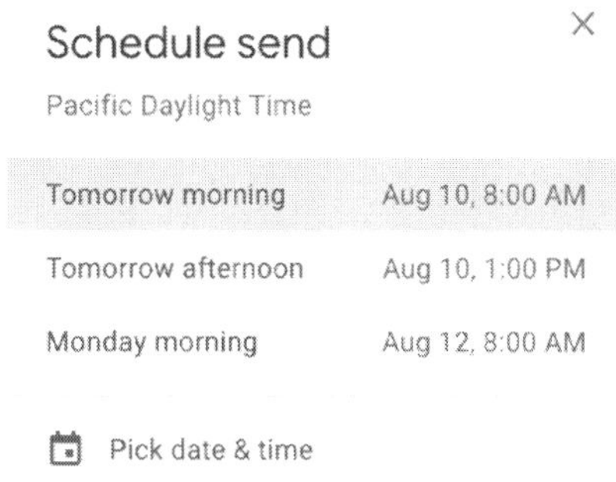

If those times don't work, then select Pick date & time, which opens up a calendar:

Pick date & time

August 2019

S	M	T	W	T	F	S
28	29	30	31	1	2	3
4	5	6	7	8	9	10
11	12	13	14	15	16	17
18	19	20	21	22	23	24
25	26	27	28	29	30	31
1	2	3	4	5	6	7

Aug 9, 2019

9:29 PM

Cancel Schedule send

HOW TO READ EMAIL

A lot of people get an email, open an email, and reply to email. Sound familiar? There's so much more you can do to organize your inbox and be more productive.

The inbox is that big area in the middle of your screen. If you just started, then you probably have an email from Andy from Google:

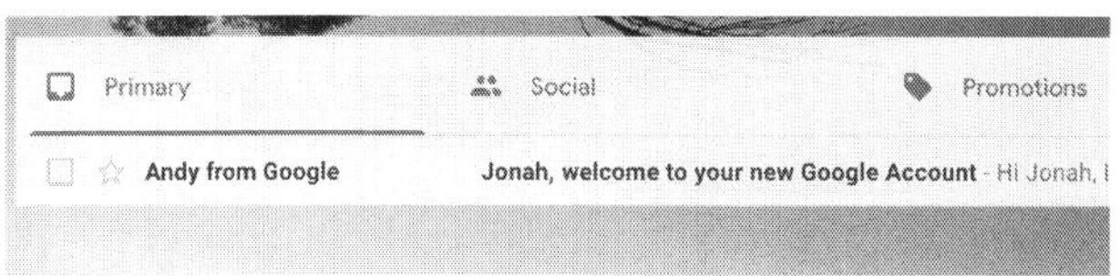

Above that are three tabs: Primary (where most of your email is), Social (friend requests and things pertaining to social networks), and Promotions (offers from companies you subscribe to). If someone swears up and down that they sent you an email and you don't see it in your Primary tab, then check Spam (in the menu to your left) or one of those tabs:

Not a fan of tabs and want to get rid of them? Or you are a fan and you want more? We are going to cover this soon when we talk about settings, but for now, click on Social. Near the bottom of your screen there's a message about the tab being empty, and how you can add or remove the tab. Click that blue inbox settings button:

Your Social tab is empty.

Emails from social networks, media-sharing sites, dating services and other social sites will be shown here.

To add or remove tabs click inbox settings.

You'll notice there are three tabs with checkmarks. Those are your active tabs. You cannot uncheck primary, but you can check or uncheck anything else. Once you make your selection, hit the Save button:

Select tabs to enable

Primary
Social
Promotions
Updates
Forums

Choose which message categories to show as inbox tabs. Other messages will appear in the Primary tab

Deselect all categories to go back to your old inbox.

Starred messages

Include starred in Primary

Cancel Save

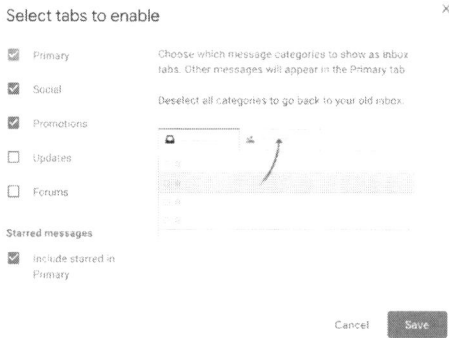

Click anywhere on the email you want to open. The top portion of the email is your main menu. The first button (the arrow) will get you back to your inbox; you can also get there by clicking on the Inbox link on the left menu. These menu options are also available in your Inbox when you click the check box on any of the messages:

The first three buttons on the menu are the email options. Let's say you've read the email—now what? You can either archive it (the down-arrow button), report it as junk (the ! button), or delete it (the trashcan button). If you don't do any of these three things, then the email will remain in your inbox. If you archive it, it will go to the folder marked All Mail—it will no longer show in your inbox. If you mark it as junk, then it goes in the folder marked Spam, which is eventually emptied automatically if you don't do it. If you delete it, it goes to your Trash folder, but, like Spam mail, it's not gone for good. You have thirty days to remove it.

If you accidently delete something or mark it as Spam, then go to the folder (either Spam or Trash), check the box next to the email, and select the button with the folder and right arrow:

Once you press that, it will ask you where you want to move the email to:

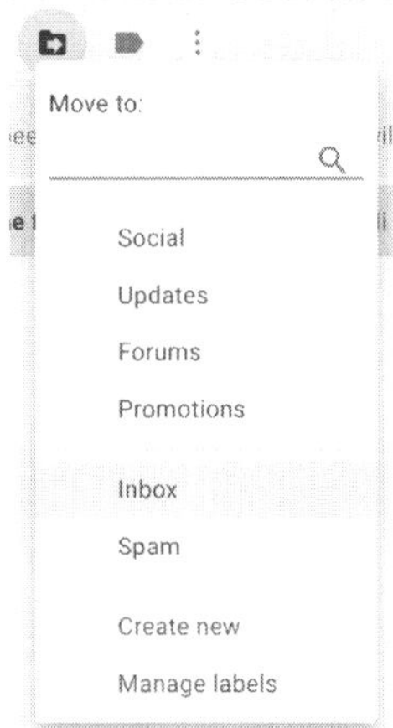

When you return to your inbox, you'll notice that the email is no longer bold. That's because it's been read. If you select the button with the mail symbol on it, it will mark it as unread. If you press the button with the clock, it will snooze it. Snooze means it will move it out of your inbox for a set period of time, and then move it back in at its designated time. I use this feature a lot for reservations and appointments. I schedule those emails to move back into the inbox on the day of the event, so it's easy to find. If you snoozed a message, but want to unsnoozed it, just go into the Snooze folder and follow the steps above for moving trash back into the inbox.

You already learned what the next button does—it moves the mail to another folder. Just like you can move trash or junk back into your inbox, you can also add new mail into another folder. The last button is the Label button:

ADDING LABELS

When you click the label button, it shows you all the labels already created. If you want to create a new one select Create New (you can also go into Manage Labels to edit or delete one that you have already created):

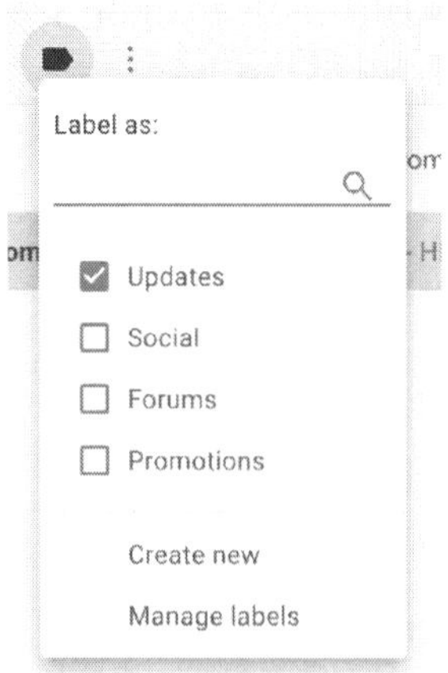

Next, enter the name. There's an option to "Nest a label under:" This doesn't work until you have created at least one custom label (those four that Google created don't count).

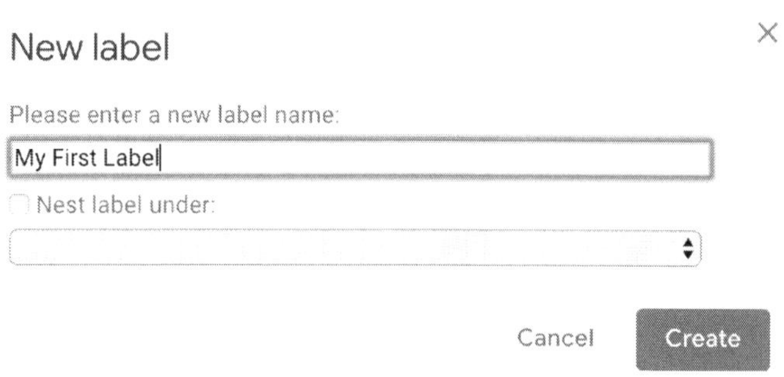

Once it's created, return to your inbox and you'll see the email now has the label name next to it:

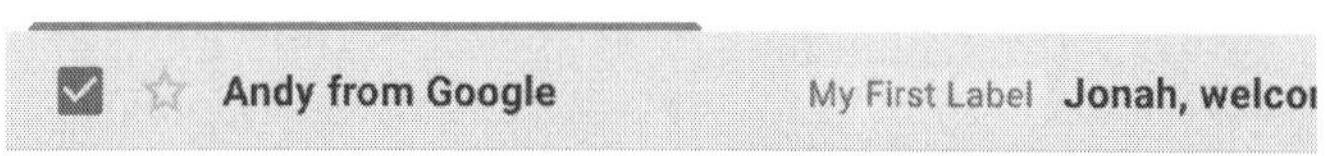

You can see all messages with that label by clicking on the label from the left menu:

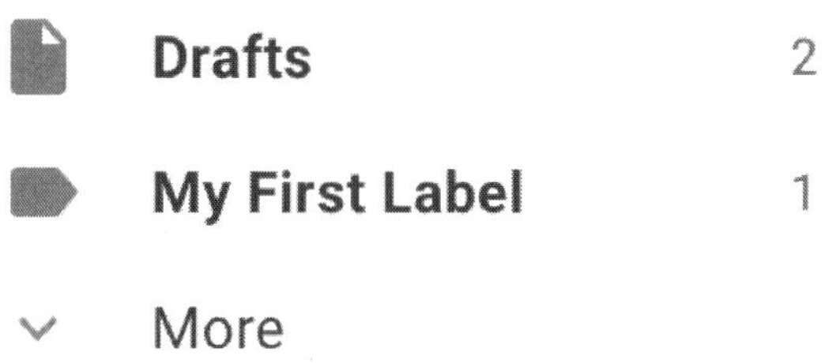

MORE EMAIL OPTIONS

At the end of the menu is the button with three dots. This brings up some of the less commonly used features. We will cover most of them later in the book:

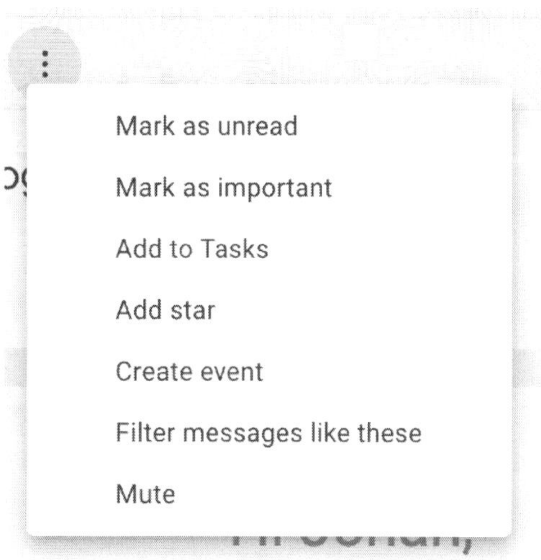

The 1 of 1 (it varies depending on the number of emails you have) with the arrow keys lets you go through emails without going back to the inbox. The right arrow takes you to the next email and the left goes back to the previous:

The keyboard changes the language of the email. This is helpful if you are replying to an email in another language. Click Input Tools Settings and you'll see dozens of different languages:

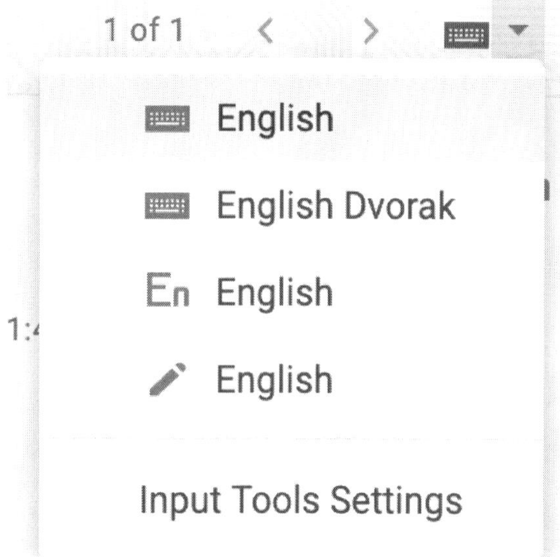

The Configure button will be discussed as we get to each of these features:

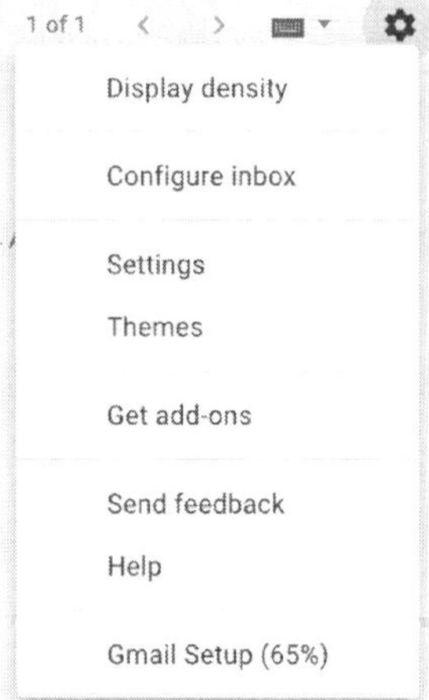

In the body of the email itself, there are a few things to note. First, if you hover over the sender's name, you can add them to your contacts, set up a calendar event with them, or email them a separate email:

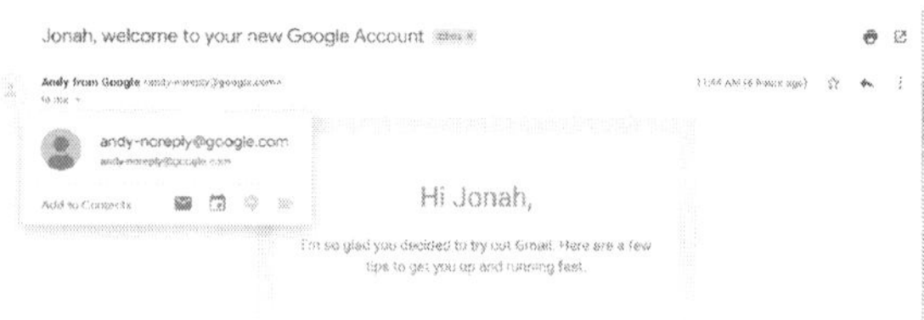

On the right side of the message, there are several things you should note. The first is the time; this tells you when an email arrived (not when you opened it):

11:44 AM (6 hours ago)

Next to that is the star. By default, all emails have no star. Stars help you organize your mail, and make important emails stand out. You can have a folder with 100 emails, and filter it by only Starred emails (which you should have less of).

Next to the star is the reply button:

And next to the reply is a button with three dots. This gives you a long list of different options—most you will never use:

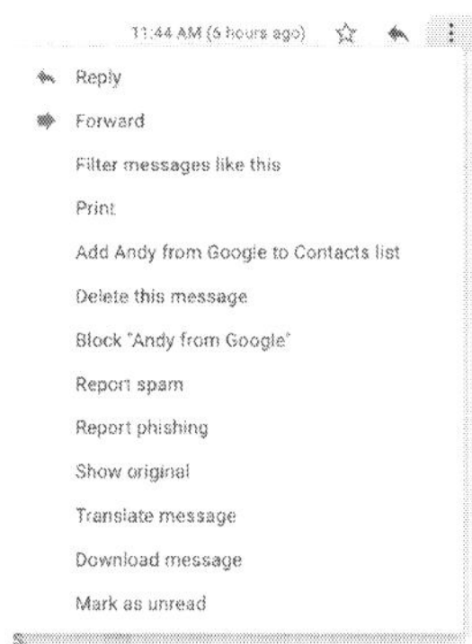

At the bottom of the email are two additional buttons: to Reply or Forward the message:

When you reply, it looks just like composing an email, but the person's name and the subject is already there, and the email is at the bottom of the original message—not like a popup box (as it is when you compose a new message):

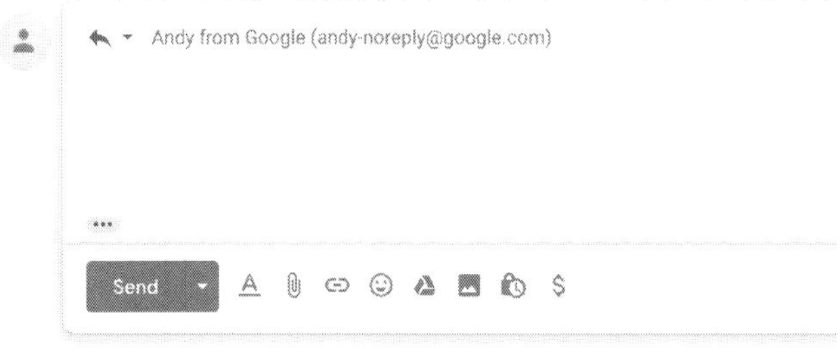

Forward looks similar, but there's a place to type in a recipient under "To":

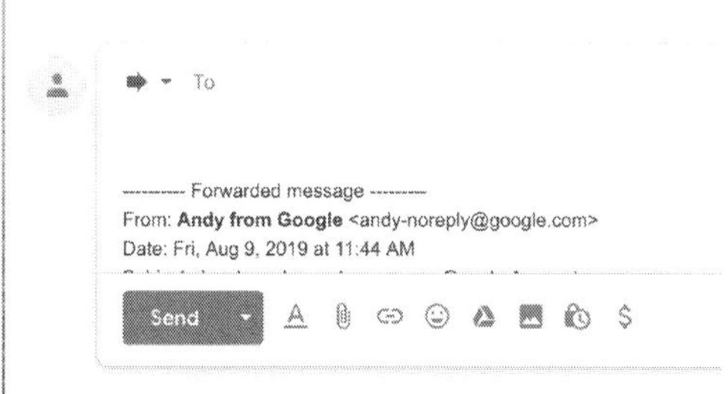

ADDING CONTACTS

Now you are ready to email someone new. Go over to the side to your contacts. Where is it? Exactly! Gmail doesn't have a dedicated place for contacts in the app. When you type someone's name, it will predict what you are typing and pull the contact up. But how do you add a contact?

You have to go to a separate website: contacts.google.com. Here you can import, export, and lots of other things. We'll be focusing on the most important thing: adding a contact:

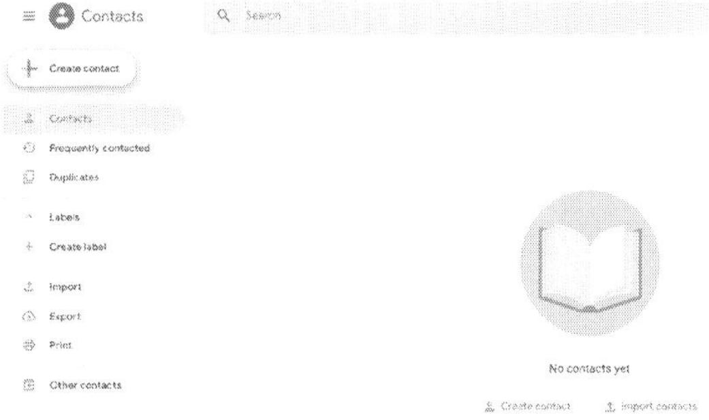

Click the Create contact button:

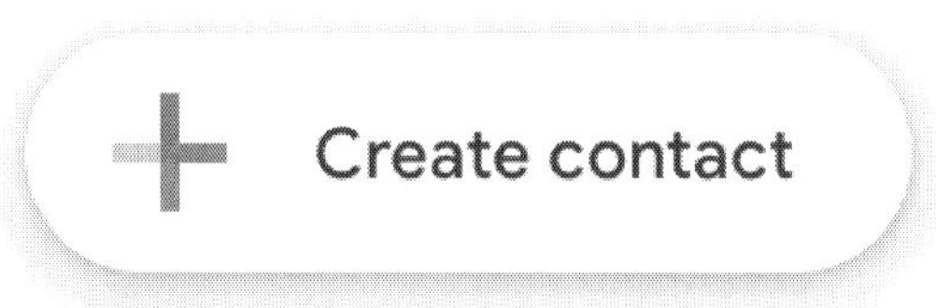

This gives you several things you can add:

Not comprehensive enough?! Click More fields:

Create new contact

Prefix

First name

Middle name

Last name

Suffix

Phonetic first

Phonetic middle

Phonetic last

Nickname

File as

Company

Less fields

Cancel

Save

I'm going to add one for my very good friend with an unfortunate name: John Doe. I can create a label for him so I know if he's a work friend or family member:

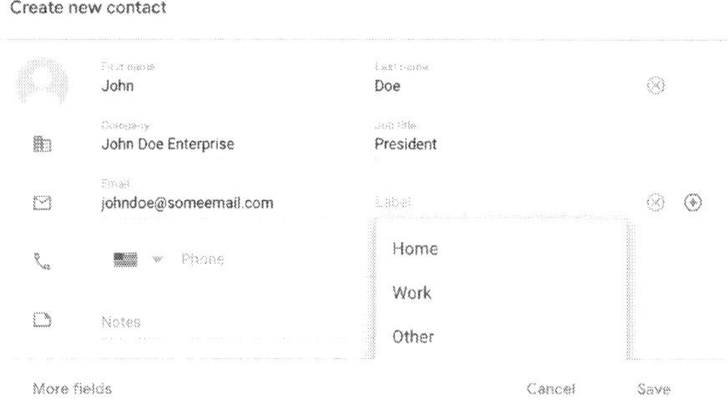

Once I save it and click his name from my contact list, it displaces everything you have inputted about good old John. You can even click on his email (I used Andy's from Google for this example) and it will open the email right up:

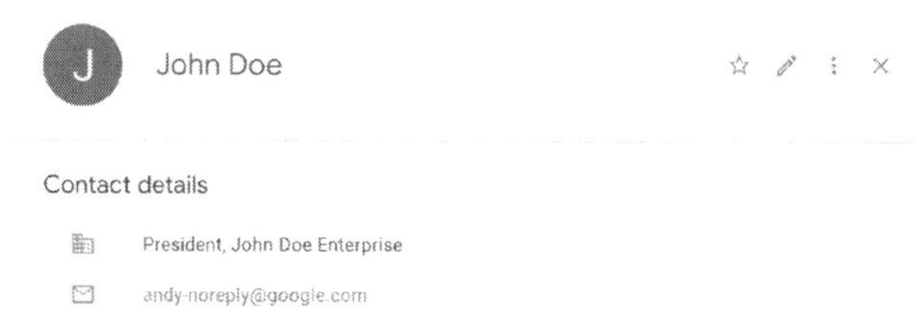

SEARCHING MAIL

Finding email is pretty easy with Google. You can simply search for a keyword like "budget":

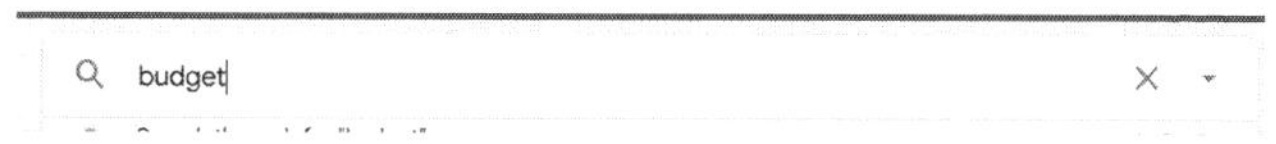

Or you can click the arrow next to the search box and have more details. You can search for the word "Budget" but tell Gmail that you only want to see emails from a certain person, sent on a certain date, and it included an attachment:

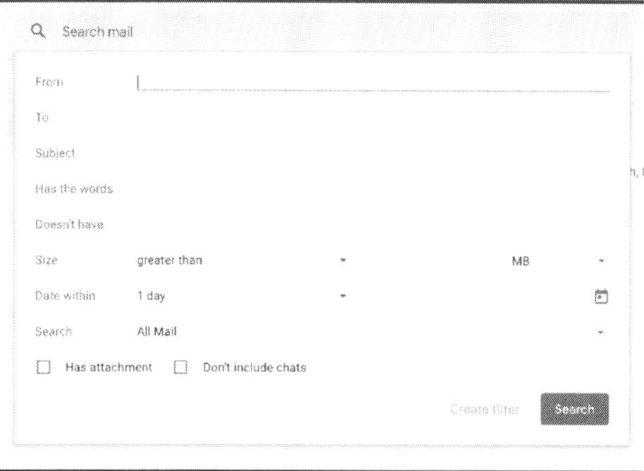
Search mail
From
To
Subject
Has the words
Doesn't have
Size
greater than
MB
Date within
1 day
Search
All Mail
Has attachment
Don't include chats
Create filter
Search

[3]

Chats and Phone / Video Calls

This chapter will cover:

- Chat messing in Gmail
- Making / receiving calls in Gmail
- Google Hangouts

Email is cool, but today people are all about real-time answers. That's where Google Chat and Hangouts become important.

These tools are both in the same place. Chat is like an instant message and Hangouts is a video call. To get started with either, go to Start a new one below the conversations icon:

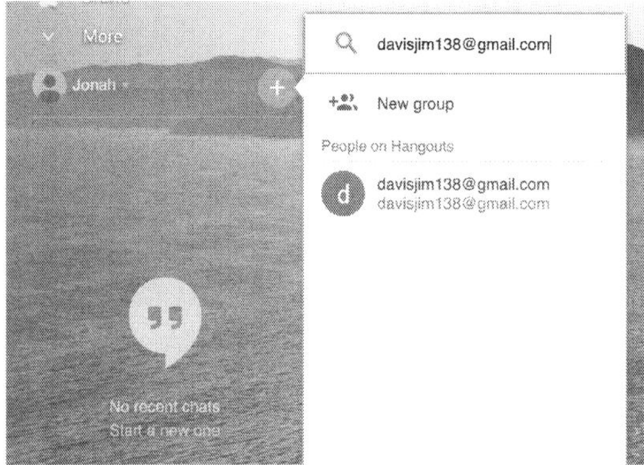

After your first Hangout, it will show you've had a conversation already:

To start a new one, just click the + sign as in the image below:

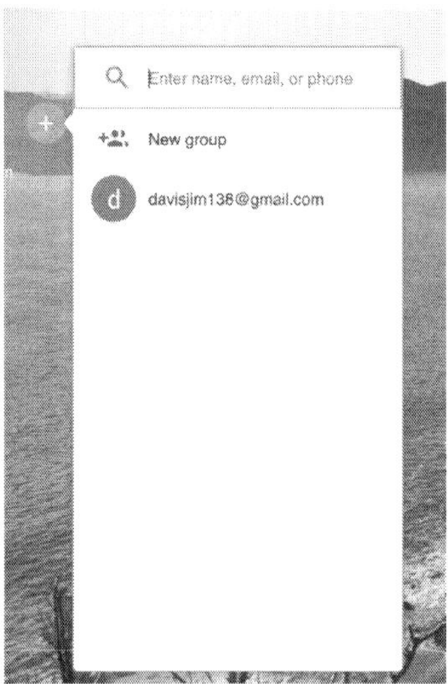

You can also bring this up with the menu bar on the very bottom left side of your screen. Here, I'll point out one icon you should know: the phone:

When you click that, you can make a free phone call right from your browser! There's not a lot to it, so I won't cover it in detail. Add the number you want and hit enter. That's it! When a person gets the call, it will say unknown. If you want your own personal Google number, then hit the + next to the $0.00. It will walk you through the steps to get a number. Why does it say $0.00 if it's free? Because it's only free within the U.S. and Canada. If you call outside that, there is a cost—albeit a low one. Some countries cost $0.01 a minute, some more remote, undeveloped countries cost over $1 a minute.

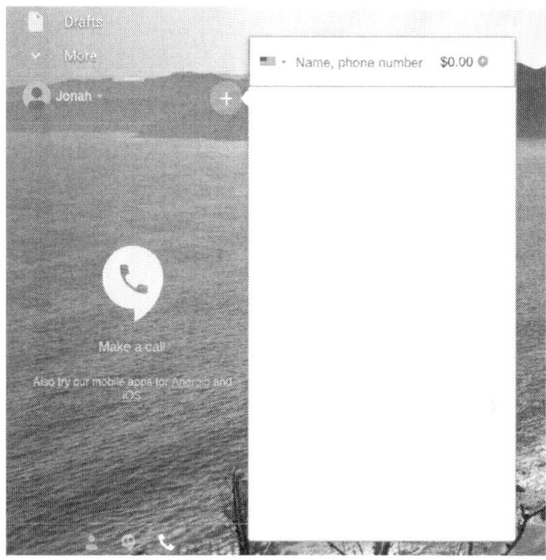

Back to Chat/Hangout; once you type in a valid email, it will open a box where you can begin the conversation. The person on the other end sees something similar. Type your message where it says Send a message, and hit enter/return:

Want to do a group chat? Click the icon of a person with a +, then add the person's email:

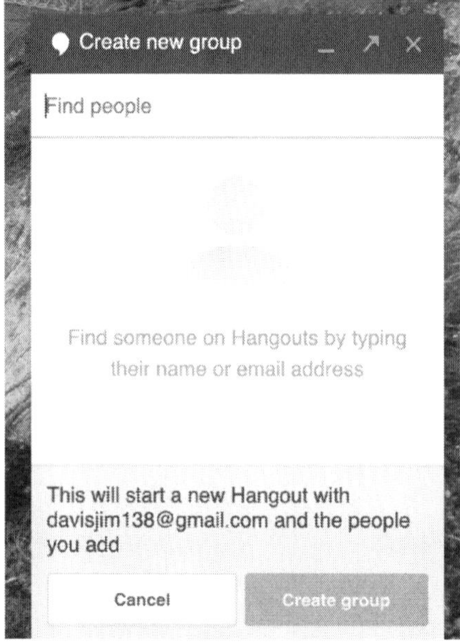

The configure button has several options such as if you want to archive or delete the conversation (if you delete it, then you won't be able to recover it):

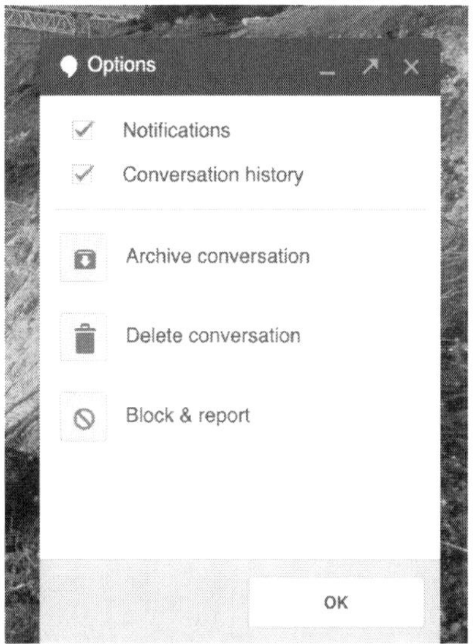

To start a Hangout, click the camera button. This opens a separate window. If it's your first Hangout, it's going to ask for a few permissions. Basically, Google is asking your computer if it's okay to use your webcam and mic:

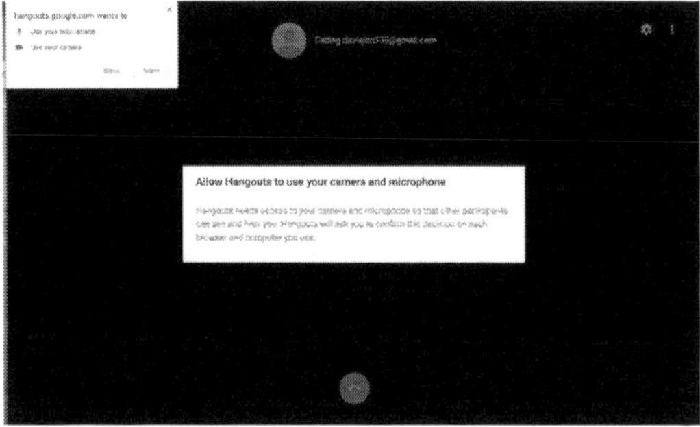

As you're getting set up, the other person will see a notification in Gmail saying someone wants to video call them:

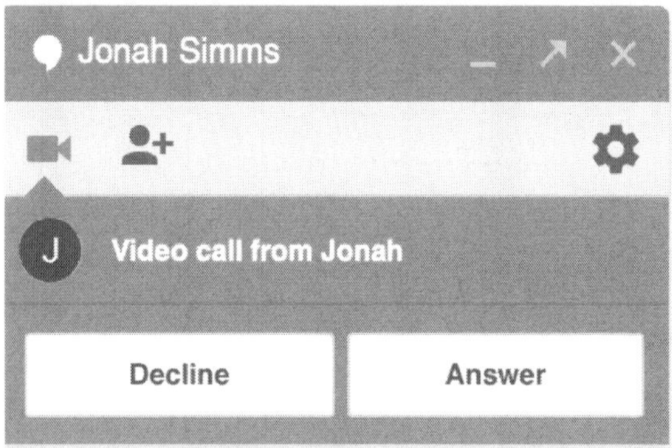

If you didn't set up your camera or mic, you can still do it while you are on the call. Just click the configure button in the upper right corner.

GENERAL BANDWIDTH

Video
No camera found
No camera found

Microphone
No microphone found

Speakers
System Default Speaker Device Test

Report additional diagnostics to help improve Hangouts.

DONE

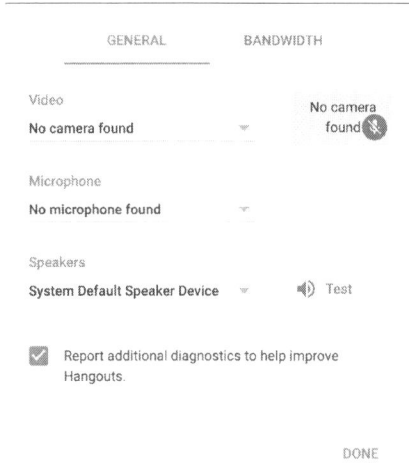

In the bottom left corner, there's an option to send messages. This is like the Chat we just saw. It's helpful if you are sending links while you are on the call:

In the upper right corner, you'll see three dots; this brings up the Hangouts option. These are pretty self-explanatory, but one in particular that you should know about: Share screen. Share screen lets the person on the other end see what's on your screen. This is very helpful when you are troubleshooting a problem with someone.

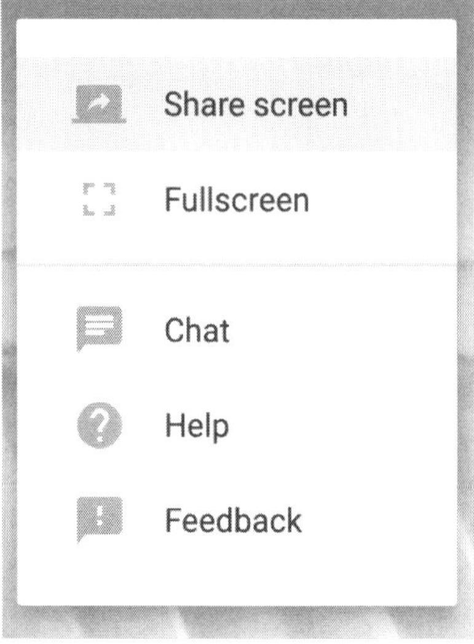

If you want to invite someone else into the hangout and have a group call, click on the person icon. It's similar to adding someone to a group text. Just add their email. You can also copy a link to the Hangout and share it. Anyone with the link can get in after you approve them.

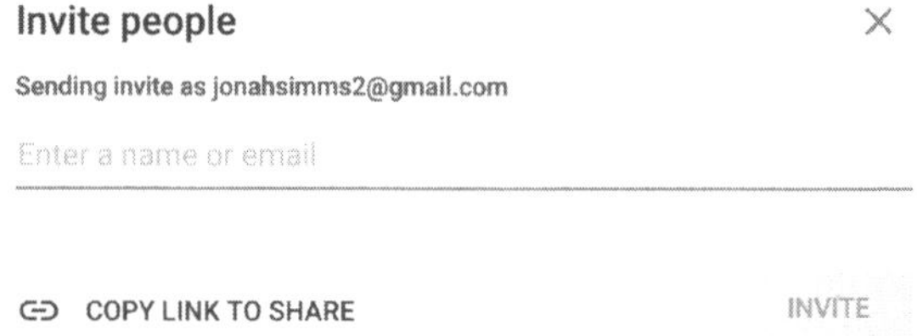

Finally, on the middle of the screen is where you go to hang up; in this section, you can also turn off your Mic or Webcam. If you are in a group Hangout, it's best to leave your mic off when you aren't speaking. It often picks up noises and Google will think your speaking and switch the camera to you.

[4]
SETTINGS

This chapter will cover:

- Changing default settings
- Configuring your inbox to fit your needs
- Adding email signature

Settings is where you go to customize your Inbox even more. We've already covered several things found here; I'll quickly reference it again where applicable.

Because this is a simple guide, I'm going to skim over some of the more advanced features that you probably won't be using; I'll cover them in case it's a topic you want to further investigate later.

To get started, click the configuration button on the righthand side of your email:

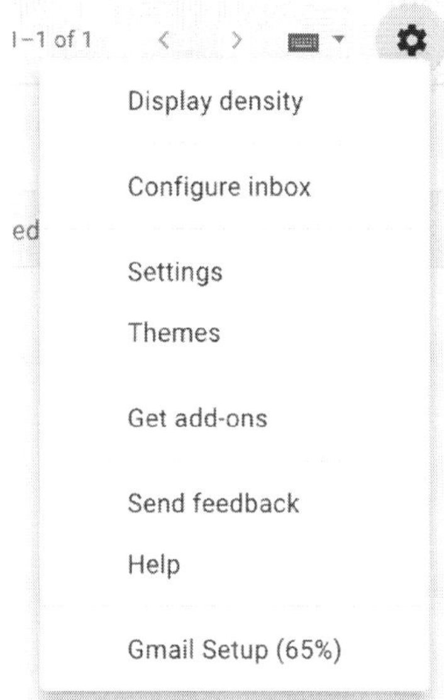

Display density was one of the first things covered in this book. This is how your inbox looks—compact with attachments not shown, for example:

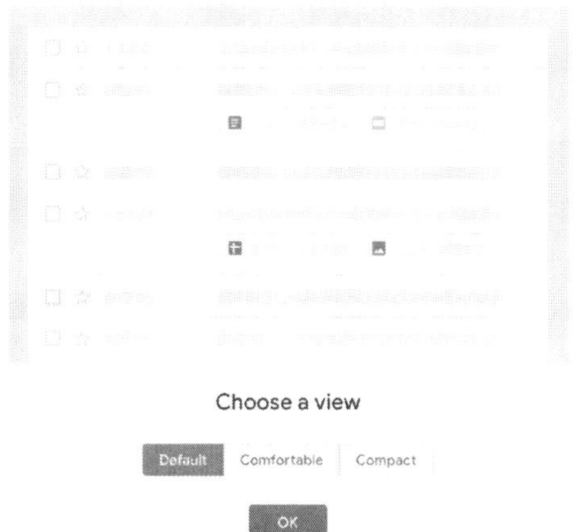

Configure inbox is where you turn those tabs on and off:

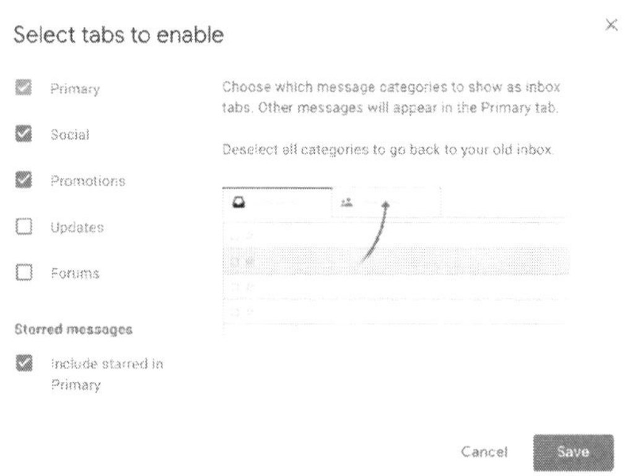

Skipping down a little, Themes is where you pick the background for your inbox:

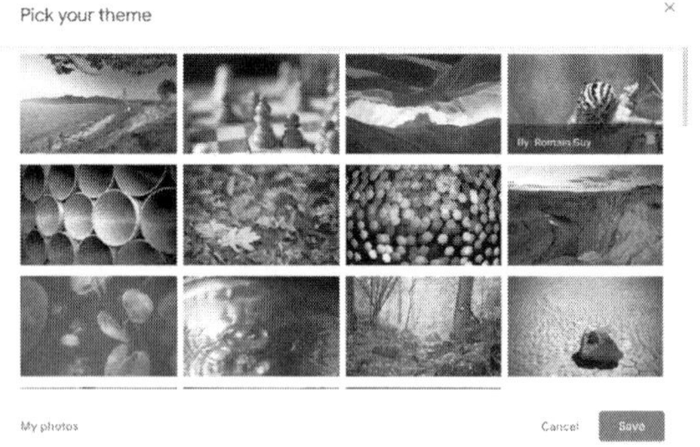

Gmail setup is that little bar we saw on the bottom of our screen when we first started Gmail; mine went back to 65% because I merely opened the setting, but didn't change it. It doesn't really matter—Gmail doesn't behave differently because you are not at 100%.

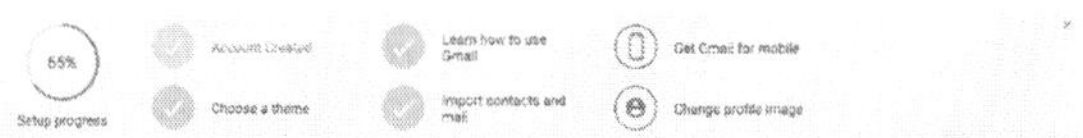

Settings is where we will spend the biggest chunk of our time in this chapter. When you click Settings, you'll see a menu at the top of your Inbox with a lot of options.

Let's start with the first menu: General. This is where you'll change things like the language and the style of your emails. There's a lot here you will not use. We'll look at some of the things you might use.

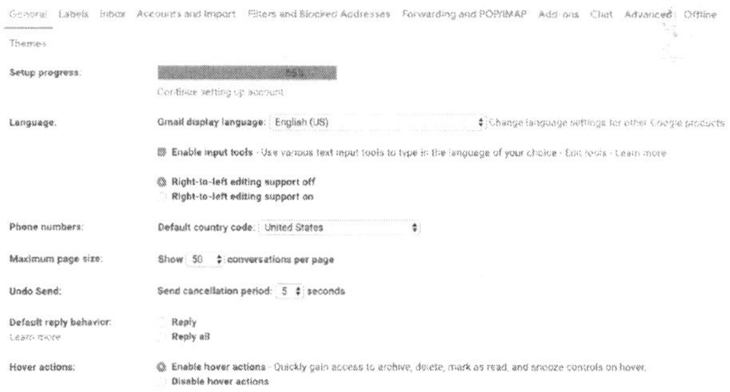

Default text style is the font, font size, and font color you use in your email. Let's say you love the color red and want big fonts. You could manually change this for every email you send, but you can also make the change here and every email you send will have that style.

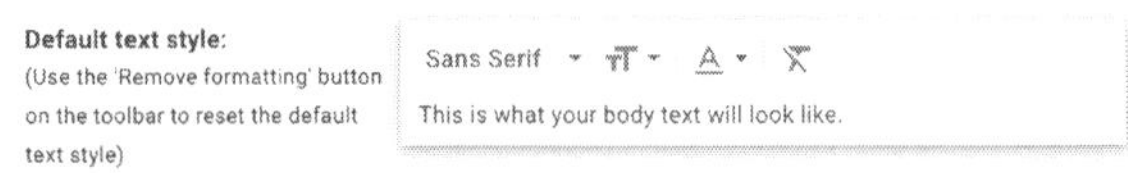

Conversation View is on by default. It groups all similar email topics together and makes it easy to follow conversations; if you aren't a fan, then turn it off here:

Nudges is also on by default. If an email needs a reply and you haven't done it, Nudges will automatically move it to the top of your inbox after a set number of days:

Nudges:
Learn more
Suggest emails to reply to - Emails you might have forgotten to respond to will appear at the top of your inbox
Suggest emails to follow up on - Sent emails you might need to follow up on will appear at the top of your inbox

Smart reply is a somewhat new feature. A Google bot gives you a reply that it thinks is appropriate. So let's say someone emails you, "Here's the doc that you wanted." The suggested reply would probably be, "Thanks!" It would show the text in grey, and hitting the tab button will add it:

Smart Reply:
(Show suggested replies when available.)
Smart Reply on
Smart Reply off

Desktop notifications allows Gmail to send you alerts on your desktop/laptop saying that you have a new email or other notification:

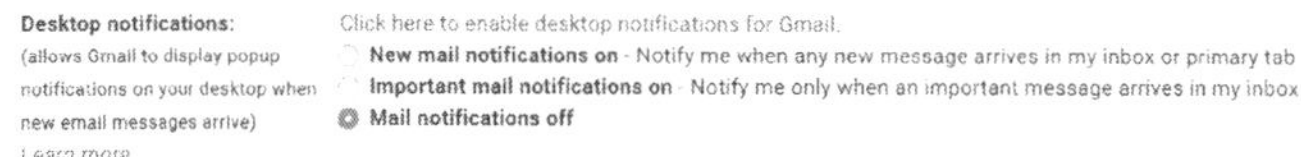

Signature is how you sign off on emails. That way if you always sign off:

Sincerely,
John Doe
111-111-1111

you could add that signature here, and every email would include it. You only see the signature after you send the email.

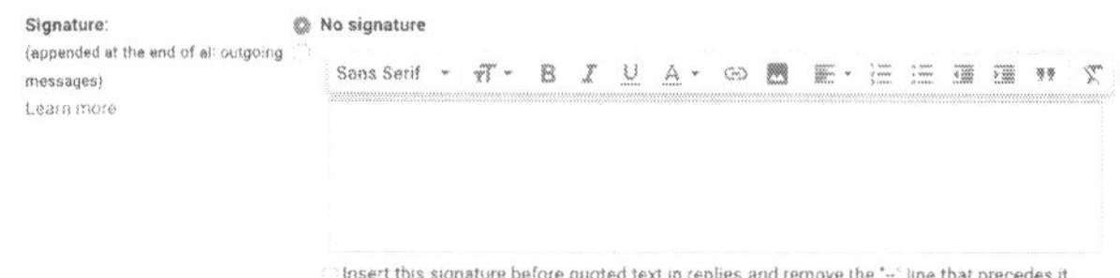

Vacation responder can automatically reply to emails saying you are away and won't be able to respond. You have to set the first day, but the last day is optional. If you don't set the last day, then make sure you come back in and turn it off when you are done with your vacation:

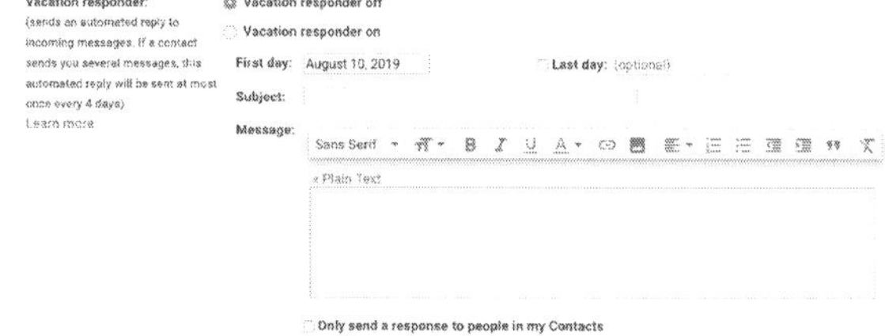

At the bottom is the Save Changes/Cancel button; if it's greyed out, then no changes have been made. Note: some of these menus have the save options and others save automatically—make sure and look at the bottom before closing the menu.

Click on any word on the menu bar and it brings up a new menu. The next one is Labels. We've already covered this section, but this is how you get back to it.

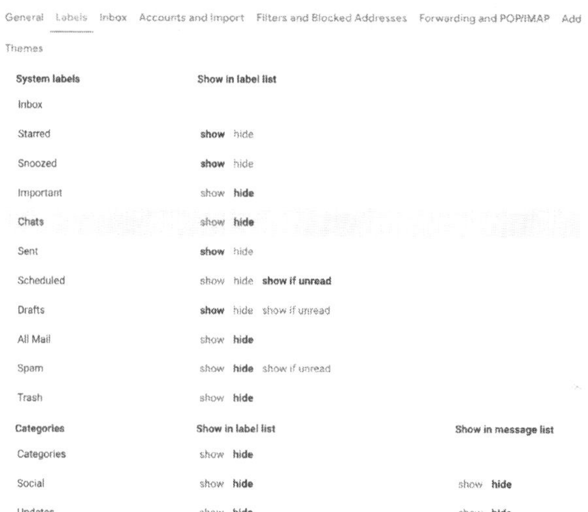

If you created a label earlier, then you should see it at the bottom of this setting:

We've also seen many of the settings in the Inbox already.

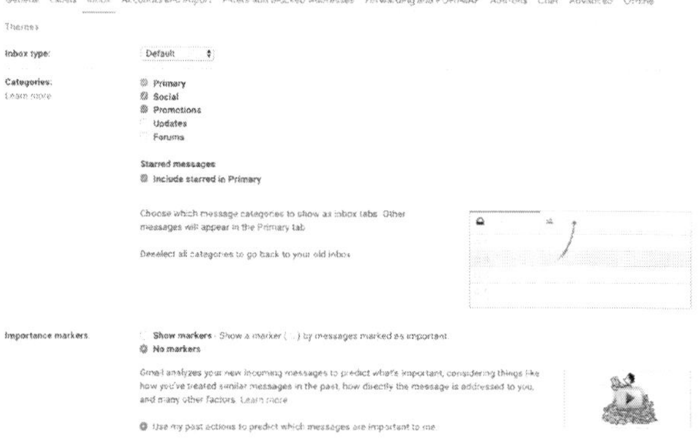

There is a setting at the bottom that changes the order of emails, for example, if you want to show unread first. That means you may have a newer email that you've already read that will be lower than an Unread one (or whatever you have selected):

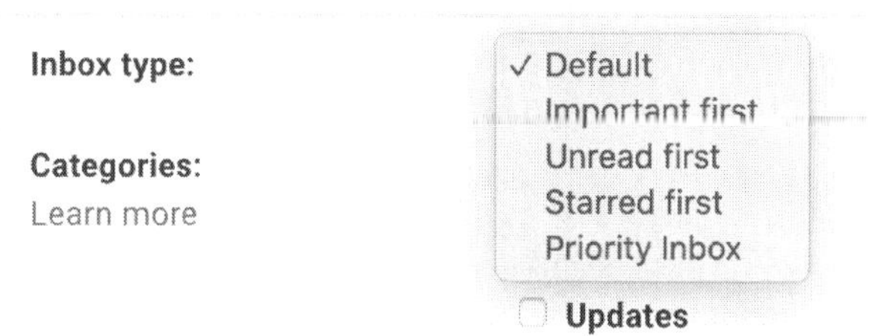

Accounts and Import is where you can go to change your email:

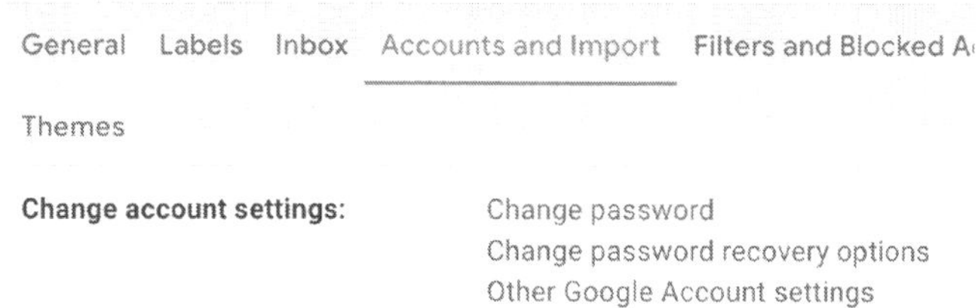

You can also change the name that you send mail as. So if you send mail as Jonah Simms, but want to send it instead as J Simms, then just click edit info on the right-hand side:

Send mail as: (Use Gmail to send from your other email addresses) Learn more | Jonah Simms <jonahsimms2@gmail.com> Add another email address | edit info

You can also add another email account in this setting. Just click Add a mail account. Why would you do this? Personally, I have several email accounts, and I have all mail forwarded to the main one. When I add other accounts, I can reply to them from my main account. So I have several accounts, but I never log into them. I have one for professional contacts; one for giveaways; one for family and friends.

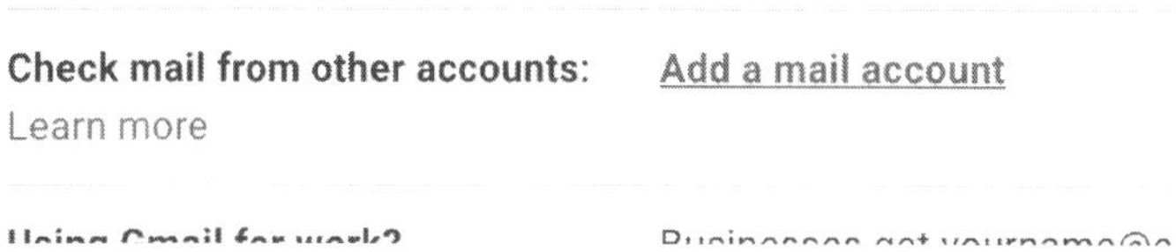

Filters and Blocked Addresses is where you go if there's someone you never want to speak to. You will still get messages from them, but they will go to your Spam. If the friend gets on your good side again, just go back and uncheck them.

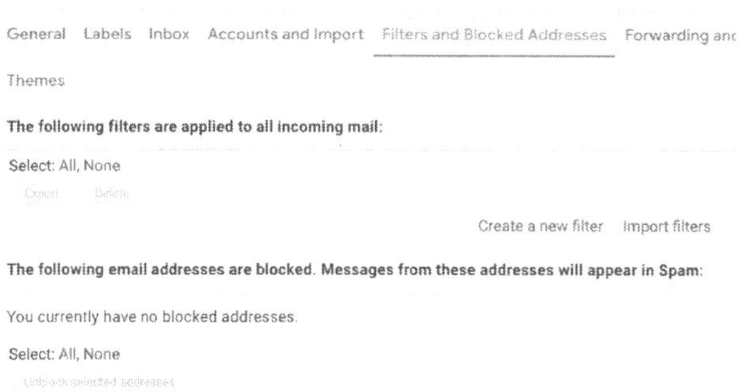

Forwarding and POP/IMAP get pretty technical. If you want to add a work email to Gmail, you can do it here, but you will probably need the IT guy's help in getting some of the settings. One thing you should know here is Forwarding. Forwarding lets you forward all of your email to another inbox. So let's say you want to give people another email so they don't know your main one; their email gets forwarded to your main one, so you don't have to keep checking this one.

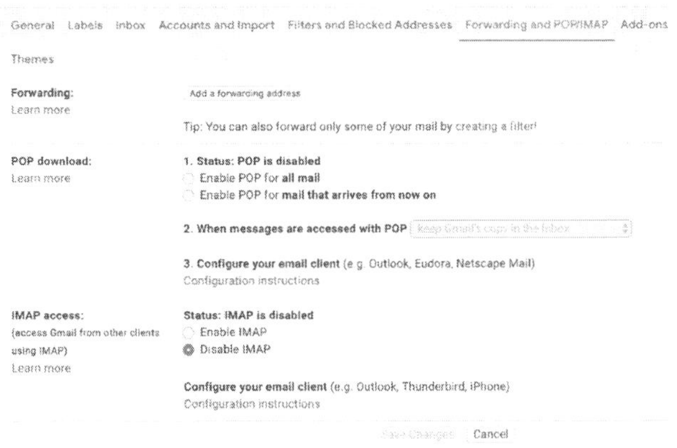

Add-ons will be covered in the next chapter. This is where you can add third-party apps:

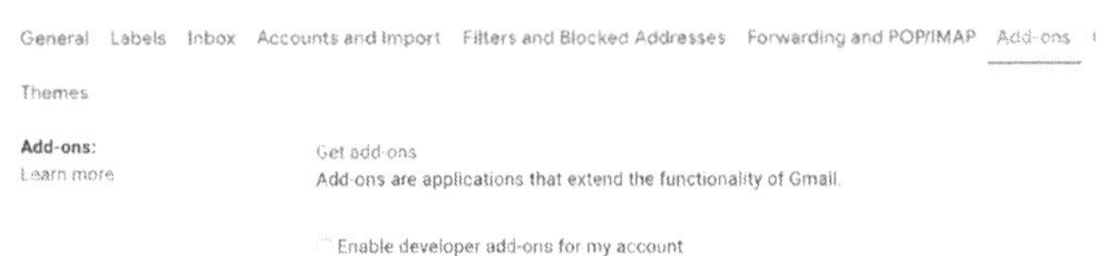

Chat is pretty straight forward. It turns the chat widget on the left side on and off:

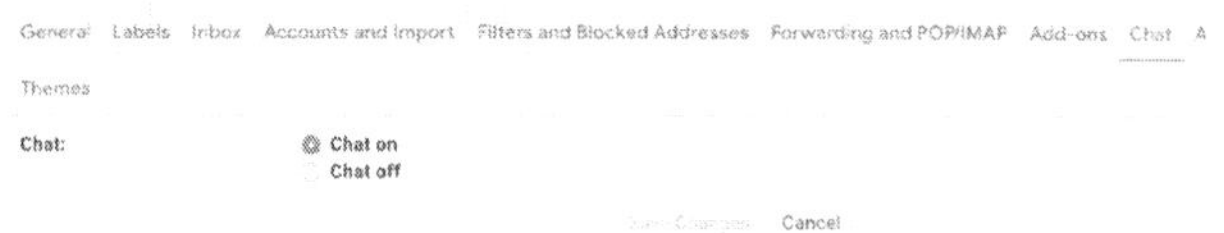

Advanced isn't as advanced as it sounds. By default, everything is disabled. If you want something turned on, just click Enable:

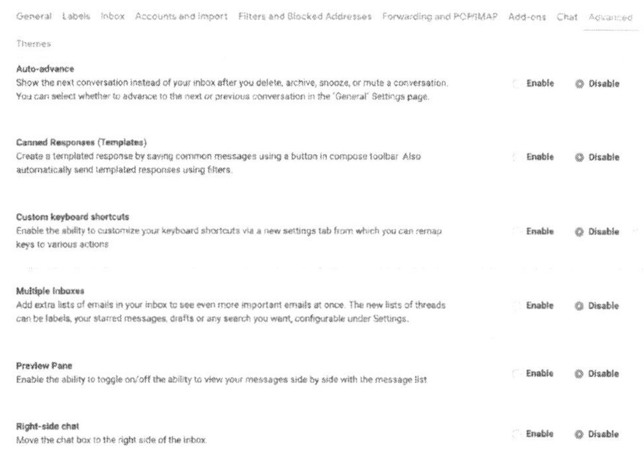

General Labels Inbox Accounts and Import Filters and Blocked Addresses Forwarding and POP/IMAP Add-ons Chat Advanced
Themes
Auto-advance
Show the next conversation instead of your inbox after you delete, archive, snooze, or mute a conversation.
You can select whether to advance to the next or previous conversation in the "General" Settings page.
Enable
Disable
Canned Responses (Templates)
Create a templated response by saving common messages using a button in compose toolbar. Also automatically send templated responses using filters.
Enable
Disable
Custom keyboard shortcuts
Enable the ability to customize your keyboard shortcuts via a new settings tab from which you can remap keys to various actions
Enable
Disable
Multiple Inboxes
Add extra lists of emails in your inbox to see even more important emails at once. The new lists of threads can be labels, your starred messages, drafts or any search you want, configurable under Settings.
Enable
Disable
Preview Pane
Enable the ability to toggle on/off the ability to view your messages side by side with the message list
Enable
Disable
Right-side chat
Move the chat box to the right side of the inbox.
Enable
Disable

Finally, Offline lets you download your email to your computer:

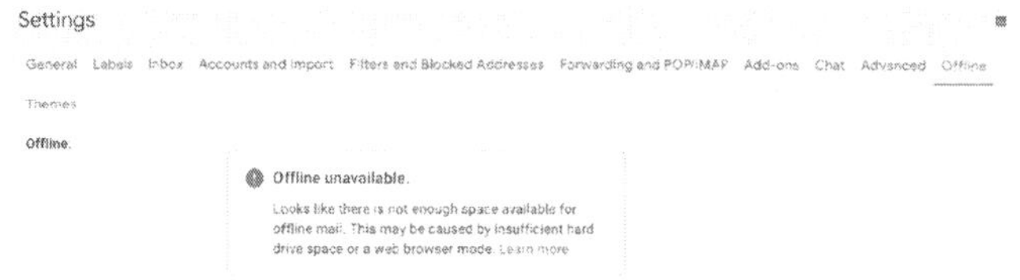

When you are ready to sign off for the day, click your profile photo or name in the upper right corner:

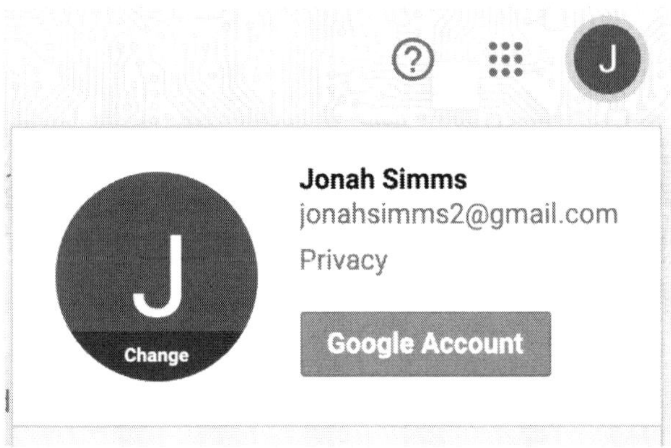

In addition to signing off, this is also where you can add additional accounts. So you can be signed in to multiple accounts and toggle between them.

[5]

CALENDAR

This chapter will cover:

- How to find your calendar
- Changing views
- Adding events
- Inviting people to events

The point of this book is to show you how to use your Gmail account; because a lot of your email is tied to the calendar, I'll give a very high-level overview of Google Calendar here. To get started, go to calendar.google.com. By default, it will give you a monthly view of your calendar:

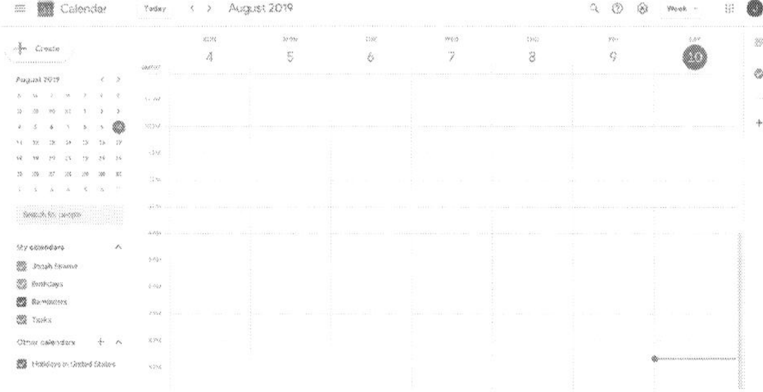

You can switch from monthly/yearly/daily or any other views by clicking on Week over on the side; you can also go to the following months (or previous months) by clicking on the arrows next to the smaller calendar.

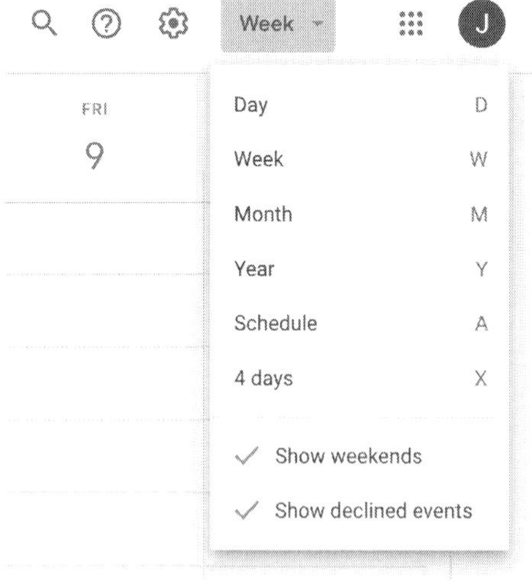

Over on the left side, just above "Holidays in the United States" is the option to add other calendars. For example, your spouse or sibling may have a calendar; they can share it with you so you can arrange appointments. This is frequently used in business when a manager needs to see an employee—they'll share their calendar and tell the employee to find an opening and create an event.

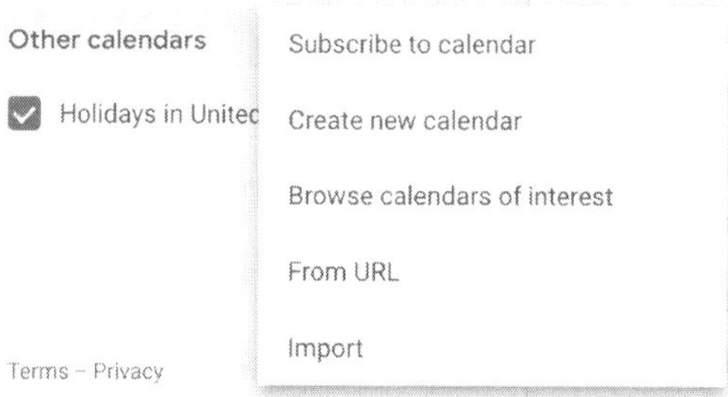

So how do you create an event? Click the big Create button over on the left side:

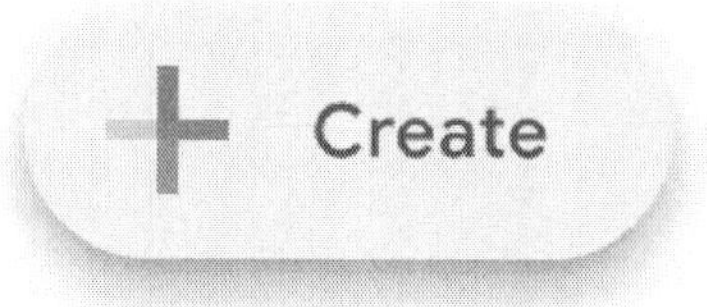

This brings up a small box that will ask you for the details. You can create it as a traditional event, or also as just a reminder or a task. You can also add a location and guests. If you add guests, they will need to accept your invitation:

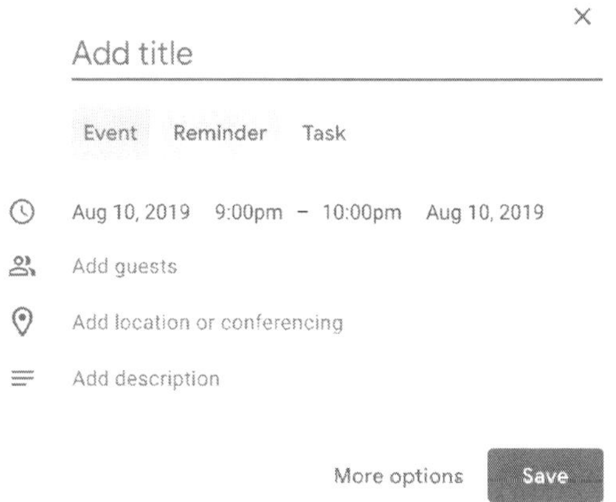

Clicking on More options, expands the box to show you even more things to add. This is what you would use if you want to attach something to the event (like the meeting minutes). You can also set up notifications, so you'll get an alert at a set time saying that the meeting is beginning.

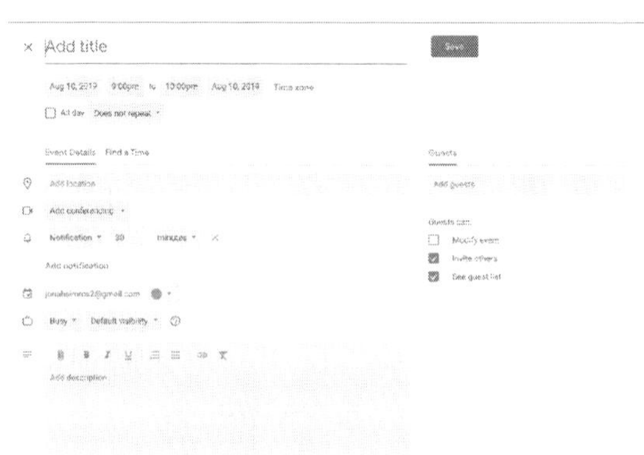

[6]

THIRD PARTY APPS

This chapter will cover:

- What are third party apps
- How to find / add third party apps
- How to remove third party apps

There are hundreds and hundreds of third party apps for Gmail. In this book, I'm not going to cover the apps you should have. It's really a preference. I'm going to cover what they are in general and how to add them.

So what are they? Think of them like Add-ons. Dropbox (the cloud-based file locker), for example, has a third-party app that puts a Dropbox icon in your message box. You know when you are composing a message and you see that paperclip to attach a file? You'll also see a Dropbox icon to attach a file in Dropbox.

On the right side menu, click the + button:

This brings up a box that shows you all the possible apps you can add to Gmail (use at your own risk!); the first ones you see are the more popular apps:

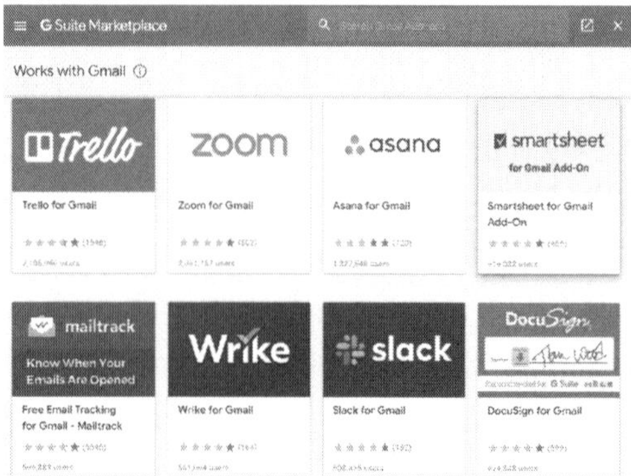

If you click the three lines in the upper left side, this lets you see all the different categories.

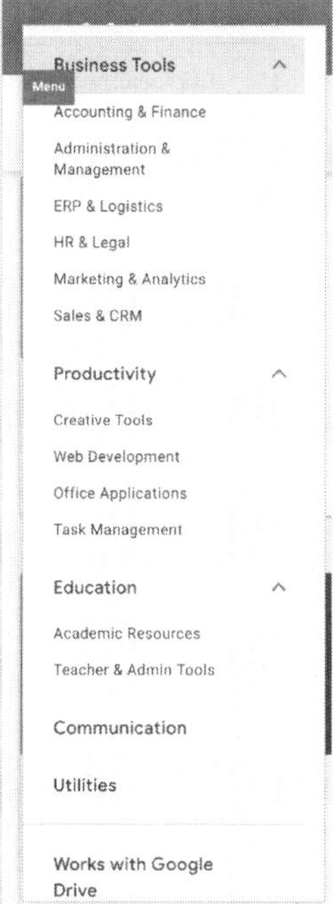

At the very bottom of the list is the Manage Apps option; that lets you remove or control the apps that you have already added:

[7]
HOW TO CANCEL GMAIL

This chapter will cover:

- Do you need to cancel Gmail?
- How to cancel Gmail

Now that you've read all of this, what if you decide Gmail isn't for you? You have two options:

1. Don't log back in.
2. Manually delete it.

There's usually not a direct reason to delete your account. If you are worried someone will hack into something you never use, then that would be a reason—but Google, being Google, invests a lot of money into security.

The advantage of keeping it is you always have access to emails if you ever need them. Maybe one day you'll need something you never imagined you would need.

If you want to delete your account permanently, then head over here—and remember! There's no recovering email once you delete it, so be extra sure before you do this:

https://myaccount.google.com

Email has settings and your account has settings as well. This is sort of your master settings. It controls all Google Apps tied to your account:

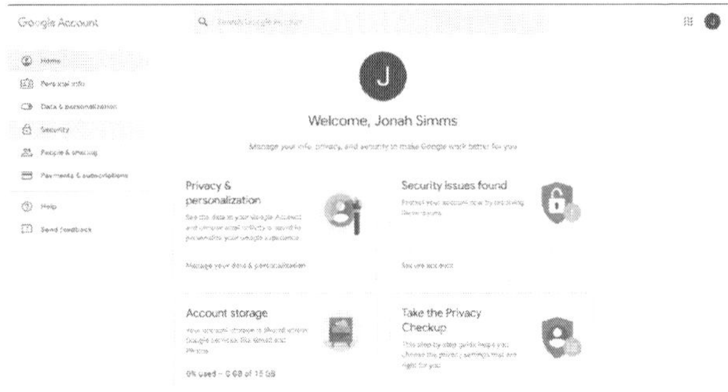

From here, go to Data & personalization:

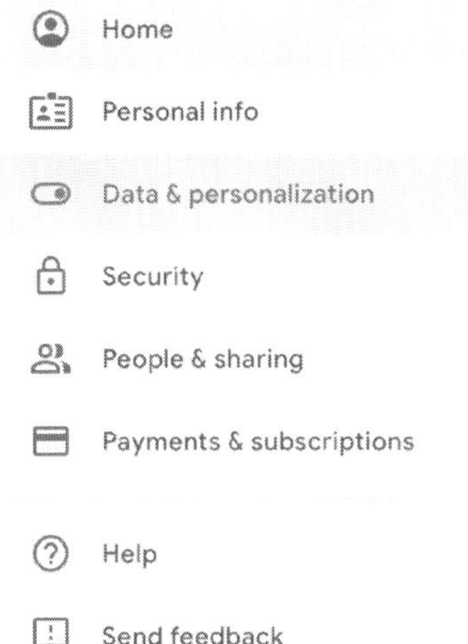
Home
Personal info
Data & personalization
Security
People & sharing
Payments & subscriptions
Help
Send feedback

There is a lot here. Scroll down a bit until you get to Download, delete, or make a plan for your data. Next, click Delete a service or your account:

Download, delete, or make a plan for your data
Download your data
Make a copy of your data to use it with another account or service
Make a plan for your account
Use Inactive Account Manager to plan what happens to your data if you stop using your account
Delete a service or your account
You can do this if you no longer use a service or your account

You can delete everything, or you can delete one service in particular—so if you have a YouTube and Gmail account, but only want to delete the Gmail account, then you'd choose service. If you want to go nuclear and delete everything, then delete your Google Account:

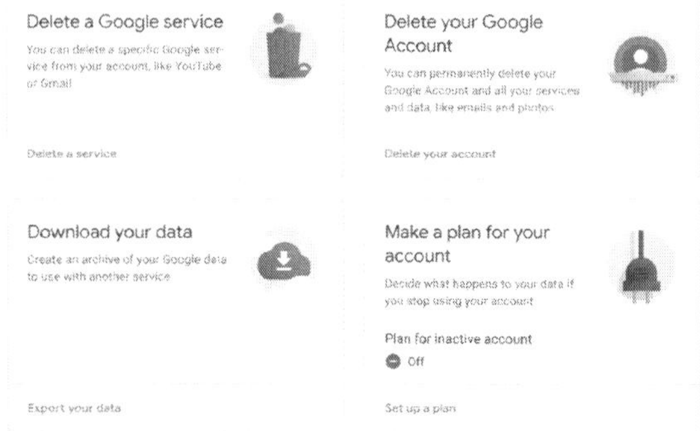

I only have a Gmail account tied to this account, so when I try to delete a service, all I see is Gmail. To delete it, hit the trashcan next to it. Do so at your own risk! This will delete your email and you'll never be able to recover it again!

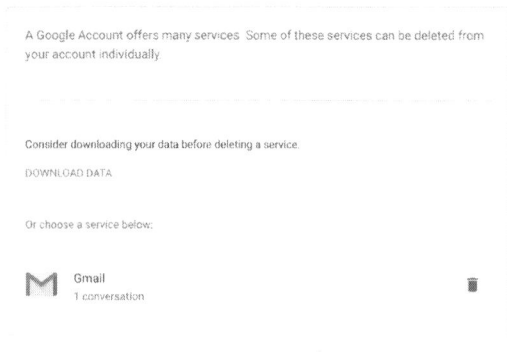

← Delete a Google service

A Google Account offers many services. Some of these services can be deleted from your account individually.

Consider downloading your data before deleting a service.

DOWNLOAD DATA

Or choose a service below:

Gmail
1 conversation

That's it! Gmail in a nutshell! I hope you'll be able to use email in ways you didn't know was possible.

About the Author

Scott La Counte is a librarian and writer. His first book, *Queit, Please: Dispatches from a Public Librarian* (Da Capo 2008) was the editor's choice for the Chicago Tribune and a Discovery title for the Los Angeles Times; in 2011, he published the YA book The N00b Warriors, which became a #1 Amazon bestseller; his most recent book is *#OrganicJesus: Finding Your Way to an Unprocessed, GMO-Free Christianity* (Kregel 2016).

He has written dozens of best-selling how-to guides on tech products.

You can connect with him at ScottDouglas.org.

INDEX

A

B

C

D

E

F

I

L

M

N

P

R

S

V

W

About the Author

Scott La Counte is a librarian and writer. His first book, *Queit, Please: Dispatches from a Public Librarian* (Da Capo 2008) was the editor's choice for the Chicago Tribune and a Discovery title for the Los Angeles Times; in 2011, he published the YA book The N00b Warriors, which became a #1 Amazon bestseller; his most recent book is *#OrganicJesus: Finding Your Way to an Unprocessed, GMO-Free Christianity* (Kregel 2016).

He has written dozens of best-selling how-to guides on tech products.

You can connect with him at ScottDouglas.org.

Printed in Great Britain
by Amazon